"Pam Douglas lays out the schizophrenic state of the television industry, half moribund as Detroit in the seventies, half vibrant as Silicon Valley today. For those of us already making television, she offers an insightful guide to where we are going. For those considering TV as a career, she offers even more — encouragement and an invitation to join in."

— Chip Johannessen, Governor of Writers Branch, Television Academy; Executive Producer, *Homeland*, *Dexter*, *24*

"In her remarkable book, *The Future of Television*, Pam Douglas takes you into the offices of the most powerful and influential writers and executives running the complex world of television today. If you are serious about working in television as a writer, producer, or executive, you must read this book. It is *the* essential guide."

— Jack Epps, Jr., PhD, Chair, Writing for Screen and Television, School of Cinematic Arts, USC

"With *The Future of Television,* Pam Douglas has managed to deliver insights around the creative and business opportunities in what has become a very disruptive and constantly changing entertainment industry. Readers will walk away with actionable to-dos and an insider's perspective on how to navigate the television ecosystem. And for those already in the know, Ms. Douglas uncovers some details around business decisions that have left us all wondering how they do that and why? A must-read for all who want to be players in the TV biz."

— Lori H. Schwartz, Former Governor, Interactive Media Group, Television Academy; Managing Partner, StoryTech; Digital Board, NATPE

"Pam Douglas has been teaching the joys and concerns of television since television, as an art form, was regarded as the red-headed stepchild of "the cinema." Now the world has come around to where Pam has always been. In her new book, *The Future of Television*, she lets us see not only where we are now — this "new golden age" — but where we are going. We are all of us savvier for her work, insight, wisdom."

— Howard A. Rodman, Vice President, Writers Guild of America West

"From the voices of top TV executives to deep reflections on the history of television, *The Future of Television* is a brilliant example of how accurately predicting the future can only come from knowledge and understanding of our past and present. Demystifying, entertaining, and intellectually stimulating, this book makes information clear and accessible to both experts and novices."

—Josie Roman, Futurist; Host, Future Salon LA; Principal, Sealight Enterprises

"Pamela Douglas offers up a vital guide map for the creatively perplexed with her clear, researched, and at times acerbic insights into the enumerate opportunities for writers and producers to develop compelling content in the transforming worlds of media. Bottom line: keep writing with passion and authenticity, and Ms. Douglas gives you tools to do just that."

— Jeremy Kagan, Chairperson of Special Projects for the Directors Guild of America; Founder of the Change Making Media Lab; Emmy-winning Director, Writer, Producer

"Packed with quotes and interviews from writers, directors, executives, and producers, Pamela Douglas's new book is not only a remarkable snapshot of an industry in huge transition and upheaval, it's a prescient look at where that industry is headed. This is a must-read for anyone who wants to work in TV now... tomorrow... and far into the future."

— Chad Gervich, Writer/Producer, *After Lately*, *Wipeout*, *Cupcake Wars*, Dog with a Blog; *Small Screen Big Picture*; *How to Manage Your Agent*

"As more and more opportunities for innovation present themselves in the entertainment industry, Pamela Douglas's new book on the future of television is a helpful guide for writers, producers, and other creative professionals to navigate the complex and ever-changing landscape of creating series for television."

— Tom Farr, Writer, tom-farr.blogspot.com

"The medium of television is changing at a rapid rate and there's no better examination of its evolution than Pamela Douglas's *The Future of Television*. With numerous interviews conducted with creators and innovators, *The Future of Television* is a must-read for anyone working in the industry or more importantly anyone who wants to be a part of its ongoing transformation."

— Stefan Blitz, Editor-in-Chief, ForcesOfGeek.com

"Pam Douglas has written a fantastic primer on the fast-changing television landscape, a topic all creatives need to understand. She reminds us that great content remains central, and the best platforms will always be those that better serve and reward all the players in the television ecosystem, from creatives to producers to distributors to consumers. Read this fascinating book to see and profit from both the changing and the perennial aspects of our extraordinary television future."

— John Smart, President, Acceleration Studies Foundation; Author, *How the Television Will Be Revolutionized*

THE FUTURE OF TELEVISION

YOUR GUIDE TO CREATING TV IN THE NEW WORLD

PAMELA DOUGLAS

MICHAEL WIESE PRODUCTIONS

Published by Michael Wiese Productions
12400 Ventura Blvd. #1111
Studio City, CA 91604
(818) 379-8799, (818) 986-3408 (FAX)
mw@mwp.com
www.mwp.com
Manufactured in the United States of America

Library of Congress Cataloging-in-Publication Data

Douglas, Pamela.
The future of television : your guide to creating TV in the new world / Pamela Douglas.
p. cm.
ISBN 978-1-61593-214-6
1. Television—Production and direction—Handbooks, manuals, etc. 2. Television broadcasting—Handbooks, manuals, etc. 3. Television series—Authorship.
4. Television authorship. I. Title.
PN1992.5.D68 2014
791.4502'32—dc23
2014018908

Cover design by Johnny Ink www.johnnyink.com
Interior design by Jay Anning
Copyediting by Gary Sunshine

ACKNOWLEDGMENTS

THANK YOU TO:

Joe Peracchio for brilliant research assistance for this book;

Bear McCreary for connecting me with pioneering makers of digital series;

Raya Yarbrough for designing and drawing The Old World, Between Worlds, and The New World landscapes;

John Spencer for all his support;

And the many writers, producers, and executives who generously contributed their experiences and insights to this project.

CONTENTS

PREFACE

IMAGINING THE FUTURE

I WAS CHARMED BY THE STREETLIGHTS. How quaint, I thought, that they still had them in this time. Oh, wait. I'm in this time. A momentary time-traveler's panic swept me: How will I get home? Of course, I reconciled myself that I actually do live in this era, and I was standing at my own front door.

No doubt I was influenced by research for this book. Through 2013 and early 2014 I interviewed heads of programming at both new and traditional platforms ranging from Netflix to YouTube channels, from premium cable to newcomers like DirecTV, and individual showrunners and writers. Television today feels like the moment after the Big Bang with creation spinning out at near-infinite speed. And the new crop of TV executives sound like they're riding these atomic broncos shouting "whoopee!"

Translating all this down to earth: more quality dramas and comedies of more kinds in more lengths will be made in more ways on more venues.

It's part of "The Great Convergence," long anticipated and now arriving. In theory, it comes from melding television with the Internet, but in practice it's so much more because this is not a mere technological change.

Someone asked if I think the new TV outlets and shows will kill each other off, if competition will inevitably whittle them down to a top few, as happened with traditional networks. Apparently not. It seems that the entities are defining niche audiences and other ways to identify themselves in the crowd. In the past, the only option was to reach the broadest audience with material that would offend no one, and that mandate may continue on the "legacy" networks (ABC, CBS, NBC, and Fox). But the freedom to program for distinct and passionate interests has freed writers and producers to make series elsewhere that would have been impossible in the past. That's been happening on cable for years, and it's amplified with the growth of fully professional digital platforms and subscription-based TV.

As for ways of succeeding, when people ask is it this way or that or some other way, my answer is simply yes. It's all of them. Everything is happening at once and everything is possible.

That's not the future. That is now. But it's such a new "now" that many people are still catching their collective breath.

And many are afraid.

Try this: Picture the future. I don't mean your job or family in the next couple of years. Imagine whatever sounds "futuristic" to you, maybe 2050 or 2100. What do you see in your city? Burned-out buildings collapsed and overrun with ravaging animals? Bizarre insects that survived a catastrophe? Carcasses of cars that don't run? Skies too dank for sunshine? The crown of the Statue of Liberty on a deserted beach? Tattered remnants of the Hollywood sign? Humans beaten back before civilization or enslaved by machines?

Whether those dystopian images result from environmental disasters — fires, floods, earthquakes, volcanoes, polar shifts, falling meteors — or wars or disease or alien conquest or, let us not forget, The Zombie Apocalypse — this horrific future has been relentlessly portrayed in movies, games, comics, and on TV.

I wonder why. Who gains from persuading the general public to believe the future is to be dreaded? Who profits from people who feel hopeless or terrified, overwhelmed by forces beyond their control? To whose advantage is it to create a narrative that the way to survive is by finding a hero with super-powers to lead or save you, or by attaining magical powers yourself, thus bypassing an actual path to power in current time?

Think about it.

Certainly the message has been well sold. Every single term at the USC School of Cinematic Arts, among the many gifted and original writers, a few screenwriting students pitch dystopian postapocalyptic stories in my classes. The cliché-ridden fantasies are usually the same. They used to mostly be knockoffs of *Buffy*, but I established a rule against shows about teenagers with super-powers who save the world, so those pitches have found other ways of imitating visions of the end of the world.

When I challenge those students to find other subjects some of them reply "but that's what they're buying." Okay, who are "they"? Sure, in our time of abundance, someone somewhere is buying more dystopian futures (*Sharknado* anyone?). And blockbuster movies that rely on special effects are continuing to push these out. But I'm telling you, at least in television, I've been interviewing "them" for this book and most of "them" are buying character-driven stories. The apocalypse is old-fashioned, guys. Not happening.

Recently, a group of scientists were at my house talking about issues facing colonists on Mars. They were meeting with my husband, John Spencer, who is President of the Space Tourism Society. I wasn't part of it, but I couldn't help overhearing references to 2020 as the past, and hearing them describe a future full of possibilities.

So what better future can we screenwriters imagine? That's difficult, right? A positive view is partly uncharted because it has rarely been done and risks falling into saccharine wish fulfillment. And since drama requires conflict, if you are deprived of external disaster, the writer has to work harder to discover drama between characters.

As a beginning writer, I worked briefly on *Star Trek: The Next Generation*. Long before my time, Gene Roddenberry had created a universe where humans would be essentially moral. As far back as the original *Star Trek* in 1966, characters were to be beyond bias against anyone's racial, gender, or even species background; everyone's motives were to be pure as they "searched out new worlds." But perfection is really hard to write into stories. In fact, to find dramatic conflict *Next Generation* sometimes resorted to infecting characters with a virus or depriving them of sleep or inhabiting them with an alien in order to change personalities enough to drive a collision.

I'm not suggesting answering dystopia with utopia. But I am urging courage to look forward.

We are in a vortex of change where all times are simultaneous. That's not only because we can download 13 hours of *House of Cards* at once, or binge on 60 hours of *The Wire* new-to-us nine years after it went off the air. And it's not *Battlestar Galactica*'s "all this has happened before and all of it will happen again" that assumes a circular pattern. And it's not only that we can instantly be on Mars through a rover's lens.

The future is an eternal now. If you try to picture the streetlights extending into infinity, the possibilities go all the way to the stars. Go with them.

INTRODUCTION

WHAT IS TELEVISION?

CONSIDER THE ANCIENT PERSIAN LEGEND of *Scheherazade*. The tale begins with a king who married a new virgin each day, and sent yesterday's wife to be beheaded the next day. He had killed 1,000 women by the time Scheherazade volunteered to spend one night with him. You see, she knew something....

Once in the king's chambers, Scheherazade told a story as the king lay awake and listened with awe. The night passed, and Scheherazade stopped in the middle of the story as dawn was breaking. The king asked her to finish, but Scheherazade said they were out of time. So the king spared her life for one day to finish the story. The next night, no sooner did Scheherazade finish the story than she began a second, even more intriguing. Again, she stopped halfway through at dawn. You guessed it: the king spared her life for one more day to finish the second story.

As time went on, the king kept Scheherazade alive day after day, as he eagerly anticipated finishing last night's story. At the end of 1,000 stories, Scheherazade said she had no more tales to tell him. But during these 1,001 nights, the king had fallen in love with her. Having been made a wiser and kinder man by Scheherazade and her tales, he spared her life, and made her his queen.

Now, what did Scheherazade know?

Well, she should've known not to consort with a murderer. Putting that aside, she knew sex sells only temporarily. But she knew something more important: the power of serialized stories.

The ability of episodic storytelling to lure audiences into a fictional world, and the power to make that world seem real, runs deep in human history. It reaches from cave dwellers around a fire to Scheherazade to *House of Cards*, and runs throughout television including *The Sopranos*, *Mad Men*, *The Wire*, and teen shows online and off. Always, compelling characters have created compelling relationships with their audience, and the more honestly, more insightfully people's true motives and feelings are written the more deeply the audience commits to them.

That kind of intense, personal serialized storytelling is the strength of television today and in the future.

I hear some people confusing television with pieces of equipment. Television shows have never been limited to the wires and tubes inside a box. Programming long ago passed from analog to digital, from antennas to cable to Internet, and from broadcast to everything else. So if television is no longer defined as a box in the living room, what is it now?

I posed that question to several of the television leaders I interviewed for this book, and here are a few that hint at the range we'll cover.

Bruce Rosenblum, Chair of the Academy of Television Arts and Sciences, told me: "Television is content. Television is the opportunity for very talented, creative people both in front of and behind the cameras to tell stories in an episodic environment. Whether stories are being experienced on a 55-inch flat screen television or a laptop computer or mobile device or tablet, they are experiencing that story, interacting with that story, talking about that story. It's the episodic storytelling that's television.

"So *House of Cards* is television even though it's delivered into the home over broadband. And the shows on CBS are television. And *Breaking Bad* on basic cable, and *Game of Thrones* on HBO. Those are all television. You can watch television on a television set or on a laptop or a mobile device, but what you're watching is the story."

Aaron DeBevoise, former Executive Vice President of Programming at Machinima, prefers the term "video." Machinima is a game-based online network of original scripted series that sees itself as developing what it thinks of as "i.p." (intellectual property) that can be explored on many platforms, rather than individual shows.

"In the past, the definitions of the content and the TV set were merged. Now they're getting broken apart. In the future we're going to look at a television set as just one of the four devices we have in the house for video. And that video can be anything from short form to long form to feature length, to episodic 44-minute hour dramas. Video is anything on any screen and a television set is one of the devices you can get video on, versus TV as being the definition of the content that lives on a television.

"The statement 'I watched *The Walking Dead* on television' is going to be absurd ten years from now. Why are you telling me the place you watched it on? You're just going to say 'I watched *The Walking Dead*.'"

Of course, that assumes people will be watching *The Walking Dead* ten years from now, and that supposes that character-driven serialized storytelling will continue to prevail — an idea no one doubts.

That compelling connection to continuing story lines has led companies that never made original scripted dramas to get into the action. It's good business because people have to subscribe to keep watching night after night. Look at DirecTV. They sell the dishes you see on roofs, right? And suddenly DirecTV produces original series.

So I asked Chris Long, Senior Vice President of Entertainment for DirecTV, what is television? He said, "It's a release from reality. It's an opportunity to sit at home and forget all your problems and be a voyeur in somebody else's life. That's the beauty of television. That's what I fell in love with from *M*A*S*H* to *All in the Family* — it was being a voyeur in their lives for that half hour. I'm not going to deal with anything else in life, just how exciting it is to be in their world. There's a solace and an opportunity to learn, identify with characters. Television is not bad for you. Television takes you to a place you'll probably never go in your life, but it allows you to get there from a little box.

"The last episode of *Sopranos* I was not happy but I found closure; the last episode of *M*A*S*H* I cried, the last episode of *Seinfeld* I laughed. I have moments of my life where I remember where I was."

At its core, our relationship to television is emotional, not only as nostalgia but as a component of our current lives. It's our reason to keep Scheherazade alive.

So "What is television?" According to Chuck Slocum, Assistant Executive Director of the Writers Guild of America, West: "Television is everything that is not a feature film."

Everything, everywhere on every platform — just as long as it's not in a motion picture theater. Opportunity is great but how are you going to plot a course to "everything"?

Ah, that's where this book comes in. Let's head out to explore the many paths on your journey to the new world.

IT'S BEEN A WHILE SINCE I'VE SEEN YOU TWO. HOW ARE YOU LOVE BIRDS DOING?
Dr. NOODLE
COUPLES' COUNSELING
E-MAIL candorville@gmail.com TWITTER.com/CANDORVILLE

GREAT. JUST GREAT. I MEAN, SURE, WE WERE ON THE VERGE OF BREAKING UP.

AND SURE, THE INTERNET IS YOUNG AND HOT, AND WILLING TO DO JUST ABOUT ANYTHING I WANT...
M.A.

BUT TV AND I HAVE BEEN TOGETHER FOREVER, SO WE MIGHT AS WELL JUST STICK IT OUT.
OH. SO I'M JUST A HABIT TO YOU?

WHAT'S THE POINT OF THIS RELATIONSHIP IF IT DOESN'T GIVE ME WHAT I WANT?
Dr. NOODLE
COUPLES' COUNSELING
E-MAIL candorville@gmail.com TWITTER.com/CANDORVILLE

LIKE THE OTHER DAY: I CAME HOME FROM A LONG DAY AT WORK. ALL I WANTED WAS A QUICK "MUNSTERS" RERUN.
M.A.

NOT THAT AGAIN. I GIVE HIM PLENTY OF SHOWS, BUT JUST BECAUSE I DON'T GIVE HIM THE ONE SHOW HE WANTED...

WHY DON'T YOU GO GET "MUNSTERS" FROM NETFLIX IF IT'S THAT IMPORTANT TO YOU?
MAYBE I WILL!

Chapter One

YOU ARE HERE

THIS IS THE DAY YOU DEPART. Your home looks nearly the same as always but the world outside has changed. Most of your screenwriting friends are packing up too. You look around at the snapshots of the era of movies in theaters, three networks, and a few cable stations, maybe a bit nostalgic. How did it all come to this?

Linda Obst, who produced movies including *Sleepless in Seattle*, *Contact*, and *The Fisher King*, commented, "Those of us who loved writing... we started saying, 'Well, where are characters?' We looked and we found ourselves watching *Homeland* and *Mad Men* and *The Sopranos*. Where were all the great characters being developed? On television. What was the water cooler talk about? Television. Things that we could never do in movies, we could suddenly do in television, so all the great writers that could sell their wares in this new market created a diaspora... and moved to television."

Writers have been transitioning from movies to TV for a long time. Back in 1974, critic Horace Newcomb wrote, "Intimacy, continuity, and history were the elements that distinguished television and earned its status as a popular art. These characteristics differentiated television storytelling from cinema."

Then television, itself, started to change.

By 2005, at least four different concepts described television: a kind of electronic public square, like a meeting place for large events; a forum for people who share special viewpoints or interests; a window on the outside world; and a gated community available to those who pay to determine exactly what they want. It's this last idea that affects what you can write and produce, and though a gated community sounds limiting, it's one of the sounds of creative freedom. I'll explain.

Once upon a time, not long ago, television writers had to appeal to mass audiences with what Paul Klein, former CBS VP of Programming, called "Least Objectionable Programming." "LOP" not only prevented creators from airing dirty words and nudity, but more significantly, the policy constricted the kinds of characters you could create and interfered with honestly depicting how people live and relate to each other.

Consider the moment in the pilot of *House of Cards* where the main character kills a dog. It's a perfect metaphor for how Congressman Francis Underwood will act with humans later in the series, but no traditional network would have permitted it.

LOP shows do continue on traditional networks (and working on those shows is still an option for writers). But by the mid-2000s, U.S. television became more like publishing, where magazines are customized for readers with specific interests. The parallel shift in television happened when economics met up with technology.

Back in the network era, with limited screen real estate — only three hours of prime time on only three or four channels — everyone had to watch what was available and the competition was all about massive numbers. Two evolvements changed that: Advertiser-sponsored outlets (including cable) realized that large numbers of viewers were not as valuable as desired viewers — niche fans who were more likely to buy the products being advertised. It's logical: What's better, one viewer in 100 buying your fancy car or two people out of ten who are watching the show driving off in it? Allegiance to a show by its few adoring fans might also translate into warm-and-fuzzies for a product, advertisers figured. But advertising explains only part of the metamorphosis.

Subscriptions turned everything around. Suddenly people could watch quality original shows with no ads at all, whoopee! Thus spoke HBO, Showtime, Starz, Netflix, and others. You pay for what you want. And those outlets don't care if you want everything they run — you only have to want something enough to subscribe. Personally, I'm happy to pay my $8.99 per month for the joy of seeing *Orange Is the New Black* and other

Netflix originals even if I rarely check out their catalog, and even if they make a flop.

Tiny passionate audiences have power now. In her book *The Television Will Be Revolutionized*, scholar Amada D. Lotz analyzed: "In the new environment consisting of fragmented audiences and niche-programming strategies, edgy programming produced in clear affront to some viewers can more than succeed: it can become particularly attractive to certain advertisers and accrues value from distinguishing itself so clearly in the cluttered and intensely competitive programming field."

Lotz summarized the overall changes in the first decades of the 21st century: "Different business models led to different funding possibilities; different funding possibilities led to different programming; different programming redefined the medium's relationship with viewers and the culture at large."

That's great news for you as a creator. Don't believe people who tell you to water down your material. Write with honesty and courage, not just because that's good for you as an artist; suddenly it may be practical, too.

But are we all permanently separated in our shrinking bubbles? Well, an opposite trend is happening at the same time. While we are identifying with our separate tribes, we are paradoxically interacting more within our tribes. Beth Comstock, President of Digital Media at NBC Universal, observed: "In the digital age, community is all about gathering people with shared interests and giving them a platform to interact with each other, to engage in relevant content and to create something new."

That raises an issue we'll talk about later in this book: How do show creators deal with "transmedia" and make stories that cross platforms and cultures? We all know, by now, that the shared warmth of the "electronic hearth" (as television was called in the 20th century) has diminished. That is, the time when a nation felt unified because everyone was watching the same program at the same time is over (except for major events like sports, significant news, and a very few shows). But there's a new version of community where people connect across the globe by nothing more than shared tastes or interests. In effect, these are larger tribes. As the old connections are lost, new communities are forming that are even more potent. In the future, how will you create for a community that is no longer described by time or place? Well, take a breath, and look at how television has morphed to fit its space before.

HOW WE GOT HERE

Television has always opened new creative possibilities, and has always moved forward through content. As *Wired* magazine observed, "Some of the very first programs were created so networks would have something to air between soap commercials; HBO came up with ambitious series like *The Sopranos* because it wanted to attract more subscribers. Now Netflix, on a quest to grow its audience, is…[giving] us wilder TV than we've seen before. Not bad for a company created to rent DVDs."

It's not as if we're blasting off now in a vacuum of history. Television has experienced some sort of upheaval every decade. The curators at The Paley Center for Media wrote, "Despite the dazzling pace of technological change, it is our belief that content will continue to drive viewer interest, and thus play the dominant role in shaping the future of television, just as it has throughout the medium's history. Content is the reason people rushed out in the '40s to purchase televisions sets, to watch *Texaco Star Theater* and *Your Show of Shows*, or turned to *Friends* and *Seinfeld* and the rest of NBC's 'Must See TV' Thursday-night lineup in the '90s, or ponied up extra dollars for addictive, buzzed-about cable shows like *The Sopranos* and *Mad Men*, or are now purchasing subscriptions to Netflix for *House of Cards*.…

"Of course how and when people watch will continue to evolve — the democratization of video on demand is helplessly enticing — but what people watch will continue to be driven by the quality of the content itself, just as it always has."

(We'll return to the issues of "democratization" later.)

It's encouraging to think that we as "content creators" are so important.

But outside pressures have, in fact, tightened or loosened our opportunities, throughout history. Look at the impact of:

FINANCIAL INTEREST AND SYNDICATION RULES

Take your fingers out of your ears and stop screaming yadda yadda yadda. I know you want to skip this section because that group of words looks boring, and, worse, irrelevant. Okay, it's true that while you're writing a script, no legal or business issues should distract you from living with your characters in their world. But knowing a little something about the "fin-syn" rules can help you navigate the future because you'll have insight into how opportunities can be built, or obstructed.

In 1970, the Federal Communications Commission (FCC) of the U.S. made rules to prevent the Big Three television networks from monopolizing all broadcasting by preventing them from owning any of the programming they aired in primetime. This was a big deal. It changed the power relationships between networks and television producers. Before the rules, producers had to agree to exorbitant profit participation just to have their shows aired. Essentially, the three networks had a stranglehold on the creative community.

With the new rules, gates were thrown open. Some observers think that brought about a golden era of independent television companies like MTM that produced *The Mary Tyler Moore Show* and Norman Lear's company that made *All in the Family*. Four decades later, the rise of those independents last century can offer a cautionary tale.

All along, the fin-syn rules were controversial, not only because the networks didn't want limits on their ability to maximize profits, but also because very small production companies needed money that was no longer available from networks. In the 1980s the rules were relaxed, and in the '90s they were repealed.

Immediately, media companies like Disney, Viacom, News Corp., and

Time Warner made purchases that combined studios and networks to create new kinds of corporate entities. And the networks populated their schedules with new shows purchased from studios they owned, effectively shutting out independents.

That led to where we are today when all networks have their in-house production companies and they own (or co-own) cable outlets. For example, NBC-Universal — NBCU owns not only NBC network but also cable channels including Telemundo, USA Network, Syfy, E!, CNBC, MSNBC, Bravo, The Weather Channel, and a 32% interest in Hulu. CBS owns Showtime and CW, among many other businesses. And so forth.

What does all that mean for you?

Two opposite energies surfaced in my interviews for this book. On one side, it seems like a whole generation is making videos and potential series on ultralow budgets, posting them on YouTube without any studio or network involved. Some of those shows even have viewers, and a few have sizable audiences (for web series).

At the same time, every new media executive spoke of expansion. All the online outlets own or co-own their productions. Almost all think of themselves as studios, not only distributors. One programmer at an online service compared himself to moguls in the heyday of Hollywood in the 1930s. A YouTube channel purveyor confided that he dreamed of empire.

Learn from history. The current wave of enthusiastic opportunity is still rising as I write this book. Keep your eyes open for a time when this wave might crash into corporate control like what occurred before the fin-syn rules in 1970, and after they were repealed. Maybe that sort of stifling monopoly can never happen again in this era of the Internet with irrepressible outlets and a global marketplace. But if you like the way this time of unlimited potentials feels, you might want to stay alert to where the power lies.

Now here's the way forward. The power is with you. That's not New-Age-y babble. If you are the source of "intellectual property" (that means content — worlds and characters — the stuff people write), you are in power. Really. The history of television proves it over and over.

You might be encouraged by this tale of the birth of original programming at HBO, with the series *Oz*, as told by Alan Sepinwall in his book *The Revolution Was Televised.*

Tom Fontana (the creator of *Oz*) chose to experiment "because it was HBO and they said you could do anything you want. I had written so much in the broadcast form, and I thought, 'Why not make each episode like a little collection of short stories? Some weeks, the Beecher story would be five minutes, and some weeks it would be 15 minutes. The freedom to be able to do it differently every week, and decide what order they were coming in, was very liberating from a storytelling point of view. You weren't bound by, 'Oh, I've got to get to this point by the commercial so that I can get them back from the commercial,' or 'I haven't serviced this character in the second act.' None of the old rules applied, and it was wonderful. 'Oh, you can just tell the story for the length of time it needs to be told in this episode.'"

"One of the great things about the guys who did the first couple of big drama and comedy series on HBO is almost all of them had a lot of schooling in network series," said Carolyn Strauss (former HBO executive). "They knew the rules of series television. They knew how to tell stories, knew the rules they needed to keep and knew the rules they could throw out. They had a lot of fun with that. There was a kind of spirit, in terms of going at it in a whole new way."

Oz premiered in 1997, but that description of HBO in its youth is the way television feels today, doesn't it?

Los Angeles Times television critic Robert Lloyd asked, "Has television, so long considered the lowest medium — the boob tube, the idiot box, the old vast wasteland, corporate and irrelevant — finally become hip? Is it the new rock?"

Lloyd says yes because: "Before *Louie*, Louis C.K. made a few short independent art films; on his FX series, he makes art 12 weeks a year, and it is widely seen and celebrated. The independent films Lena Dunham made are what got her the chance to create HBO's *Girls*, but TV, which has imported her sensibility unscathed, is what made her a star.

"... Like pop music, television today is multifarious and factional, and with the expansion of cable and cable's leap into original production, it has acquired something like an 'indie' or alt-TV component to complement its still substantial mainstream."

Los Angeles Times television critic Mary McNamara summed it up: "Television is the most significant voice in popular culture because that is where writers are allowed the most freedom."

TODAY'S "INDIE TV"

I interviewed Charles Slocum, a longtime executive of the Writers Guild of America, West. Through years representing the interests of professionals who write for all kinds of screens, Slocum offers a perspective so insightful I want to share it with you as spoken:

CHARLES SLOCUM

CHARLES SLOCUM: There's a category I call "independent television," which didn't formerly exist. Traditional television had to be motivated by the channel it's going to be on. But now we have the business model Tyler Perry did with *Meet the Browns*, a sitcom on TBS, and Ice Cube used to launch *Are We There Yet*, and *Anger Management* with Charlie Sheen, and the new George Lopez sitcom sold to FX.

Here's the difference: these channels — TBS or FX — did not develop and pay for a pilot. The talent developed the show on its own. They found money independent of the channel to produce ten episodes. And then with that investment, they go to a channel and the channel agrees to put it on the air. The channel is not out any money. They're out their airtime for ten episodes. They get advertising during it that helps pay back the investors. If the ten episodes do well and the channel picks it up, they pick it up for 90. Then you know you're going to have your syndicatable number. It's still a gamble on the ten, but it's independent in that there's funding brought to it.

PAMELA DOUGLAS: From the point of view of somebody who is a writer, who is not a big money person and who doesn't know about getting investors, how is this good in terms of knowing how to proceed with the new opportunities?

CS: There are different doors to knock on. You can knock on doors of people who will handle the rest of the rights. This is the way TV used to be. You'd go to a studio and they would take you to a network, back before the financial-syndication rules were taken away. The networks didn't own the shows. When the rules went away, they could own the shows.

What this means is you have an outside third party and you're not stuck with the network you originally develop it with. Now when they pass on it, it's hard to get your show away from the network you first developed it with. It's going back to the way it was from the 1970s to the mid-'90s when the ownership rules were taken away.

So-called independent TV is just four shows. They're just the beginning. But they're the beginning of change.

PD: So for writers you see a greater variety of paths?

CS: A greater variety of paths for your work to be made and get to the viewer.

PD: Does it affect the kinds of work people might do?

CS: Of course it does. If you develop it yourself and have a third party financing it, writers have a lot more freedom to do what you want to do. You're not just getting notes from a network that you have to follow or else you'll be replaced.

PD: What do you think of the idea that the Internet has far more real estate, so instead of pitching to a network that might have only one time slot open, online the possible spaces are unlimited.

CS: That's true and not true. Netflix, for example, has a programming budget. iTunes, on the other hand, has truly unlimited real estate because iTunes isn't giving you any advances. If you produce it, they'll sell it for you. But they don't produce anything. Netflix doesn't have time slots; that's true, but they don't have an unlimited budget. The same is true of Amazon because they're investing.

PD: Would you say it's similar to the days of indie features?

CS: The more you go to people for private financing, it's more like traditional festival films that might or might not make any money back. I would advise people to be realistic with your investors and let them know how risky it is. For the truly independent television mode, the lower the budget the better because of the high risk. The value of the 10-90 deal is you're dealing with somebody who will pay the bills eventually.

PD: In these so-called "independent" forms, are we following the traditional model that a writer comes up with a pitch, writes a pilot, somebody produces it, and if the pilot does well, it is picked up for series?

CS: No, none of these have pilots. In the 10-90 deal, the ten episodes are done. Ten episodes are enough content to know what you have.

But pilots are still the norm at networks. And people would argue in favor of them because you get to tweak what you're buying. And the Netflix shows are from scripts.

PD: In the independent TV paradigm, what would people do who are truly writers? They put words on pages and create characters and stories. They're not necessarily businesspeople or cinematographers.

CS: The more you want to control your future the more you have to stretch out into these other areas. The more you are just a writer with a piece of paper the more other people are going to control your future. If you want to have a career purely as a writer you'd have to understand you're not the whole package; you're an employee. The reality is that if you can't get the job you want as an employee, the opportunity is to stretch into these other areas and become the entrepreneur.

I understand some writers are introverts and they don't want to deal with all the people who are production managers, accountants, location scouts, and so forth. Fine, so partner with a producer who loves all that and doesn't have the patience to sit down with a blank page. That's the path to being an entrepreneur in a partnership.

PD: How does that differ from the olden days where a writer would go to a studio for backing?

CS: The executive at the studio became your partner. The classic examples are great writer/showrunners who work under the umbrella of a production company. We need the Grant Tinkers of this age who are going to run the company, deal with the network, and try to keep the network at bay as much as possible and let you do your creative work.

You have to be very self-aware and supplement the skills you don't have. If you're close enough you can stretch to become the producer type, but if it's too big a stretch, partner with somebody.

PD: Would you say there's more opportunity for more kinds of story?

CS: Yes. One of the advantages of these new distribution methods is they're not advertiser-supported. Advertising support creates two different pressures. One is to be as popular as possible. So you want to alienate as few people as possible and be broadly appealing to as many people as possible.

The second thing is you need to be as similar to the other product as you can be. The classic example is broadcast TV where what they have on at eight they hope is compatible with what they have on at nine so they keep the audience. It's audience-flow programming strategy. The good news is that individuals pay for HBO and Netflix. So if your base is subscribers, your goal is to have as many different subscribers as you can. That means when you have one show like *House of Cards*, you want the next show to be as different as possible. On broadcast the priority is to be similar. On subscription TV the goal is to get as many different people as possible to be happy to pay the monthly bill. One series, maybe two can lock you in for the whole 12 months.

The mandate is to be as compellingly interesting to a narrow group as you can be. Not to be blandly popular with as many people as possible and not offend anybody. Please offend some people to be that compelling to others who become loyal fans. If you can get ten loyal groups you have a lot of subscribers and you're happy. It's an opening to be more different.

PD: It sounds like a great opportunity for writers because you don't have to censor yourself.

CS: It is. We've seen this growing over the last years in basic cable where half of the money is subscription. It's still half advertising, but half of their revenue is from subscriber fees. So they have a mixed motive. That's why AMC can love *Breaking Bad* as much as *The Walking Dead*, even though *Breaking Bad* doesn't have as high ratings, but it has really loyal fans who are happy to have AMC on their cable system, so AMC can ask for more money from the subscription. They know the cable companies will hear from their loyal fans.

We saw this all along with HBO, and now Netflix, and also Starz, where the motive is to be as compelling as possible to your subscription audiences.

PD: That's a good suggestion for show creators: If you want to pitch something to a subscription-based channel, don't give them the same thing they've got.

CS: The goal is not to be homogenous. This is the story of why broadcast series get shut out. The reason cable is recognized as more creative is it has more freedom. It's not about skin or language. That's wrong. The reason they can be more creative is they don't have to be like the other programs.

NET NEUTRALITY

By the time you read this section a catastrophe might have befallen the Internet. Or nothing might have happened even after all the sound and fury surrounding the issue called "Net Neutrality." Or the whole matter might still be unresolved. Or perhaps a reasonable compromise or settlement will have been found. Before this book goes to press in fall 2014, I don't know whether the Internet will remain "neutral," giving equal access to all, or if a few telecommunications powers will charge such high rates for effective access that all but the biggest will be relegated to poor-quality signals and effectively squeezed out: "fast lanes" for those who can afford the "top tier," and slow, interrupted dirt roads for the rest.

This is scary stuff, folks. Some content providers (ranging from production companies to individual writers and video makers) call it extortion. People are also worried that control by the giants will have the effect of censoring or suppressing original content online. Your creative options might be in the balance.

Or maybe not. The ISPs (Internet Service Providers) like Comcast, Time-Warner and Verizon, are saying this is all simply a matter of modernizing transmissions and clarifying regulations. "All the better to see you with, my dear," the wolf said to Little Red Riding Hood. Being honest, their supporters argue for their right to get as much profit as they can. In the United States, the decision rests with the FCC (the Federal Communications Commission), which has a broad mandate to regulate broadcast-television stations, phone companies, and cable companies that serve tens of millions of subscribers with Internet service and email.

I asked myself why deal with this difficult subject when it's likely to be different by the time you read it. After weighing the significance of the potential challenge to people who create shows in the future, I decided to go ahead and describe the issues. Even if this particular FCC ruling becomes moot in 2015, the overall questions will continue.

Let's start with the basics. "Net Neutrality" is an idea that an open and free Internet must treat all content equally. No ISP should decide which content Internet users can see and when. They shouldn't arbitrarily block access to certain websites just because they don't want consumers watching video from a competitor. They also shouldn't be allowed to discriminate in how they handle Internet traffic, favoring one site over another.

Attorney Marvin Ammori, an expert in Internet freedom issues, explained, "If the FCC ends up implementing its fast lane/slow lane scenario, the vibrant, innovative Internet as we know it is likely to fade away. It would destroy independent creativity and it would be a lot more expensive. You would have to raise money before you distribute products, not only create them. There would be fewer buyers of your work essentially. When you have fewer companies that own more and more channels and programs you have less leverage. So if you wanted to launch a web show and needed reliable video service, you would have to go to Comcast and Verizon and offer to pay them or give them an equity stake in your company."

A Special Report to the membership of the Writers Guild of America stated, "At a time when media conglomerates are already stifling competition and narrowing options, the Internet represents a new, and perhaps the last, frontier for work opportunities. The low-entry barriers of an open Internet have spurred innovation, and writers are benefiting from new online video platforms that also give consumers more choices. They can sell their content to bigger companies like Amazon and Netflix; and 10 to 15 similar companies expected to sprout up in the next few years will provide even more outlets for their work."

"Our show got a huge boost from viewers who streamed it on their computers, tablets, and phones," says *Breaking Bad* creator Vince Gilligan. "I'm not sure we would have made it beyond the second season without it."

WGAW President Chris Keyser summarized the stakes: "As content creators, we succeed when we reach our audience. We succeed artistically because the broader the conversation between us and our audience — and the less that conversation is subject to censorship — the more we have fulfilled our desire to communicate our point of view. And we succeed financially because we are usually compensated based upon the size of our audience. Anything that comes between us and the audience in a free and unfettered Internet is bad for writers. It is bad because we lose consumers of our content and because someone else has decided which work of ours will be promoted and which will be withheld."

What can you do? First, inform yourself by googling "Net Neutrality" and reading the latest developments. As I write this, the FCC is collecting public comments, and, wow, have they been coming in. At one point, the huge volume of emails over the proposed fast and slow lanes crashed part of the FCC's computer system. After you've learned all you can you might choose to pile on.

The future is full of opportunities just now emerging. You can help keep the gates open.

CONCLUSION — WE ARE HERE

All that is just now coming into focus in the distance. We're not there quite yet. For most of us, right now, today, what is our reality? According to David Carr of the *New York Times*:

"So this is how we end up alone together. We share a coffee shop, but we are all on wireless laptops. The subway is a symphony of ear-plugged silence while the family trip has become a time when the kids watch DVDs in the back of the minivan. The water cooler, that nexus of chatter about the show last night, might go silent as we create disparate, customized media environments."

Or maybe we are all on the way to someplace new.

INTERACT WITH CHAPTER ONE

Expand your experience of how television is changing by trying these:

- Ralph Kramden in *The Honeymooners* (1950s), Archie Bunker in *All in the Family* (1970s), and Homer Simpson in *The Simpsons* (running since 1989), can be seen as a continuum of a certain kind of character. Create a contemporary character that reinterprets this role in current time on any platform.
- Watch pilots of *Oz* (HBO, 1997) and *Orange Is the New Black* (Netflix, 2013). Both are prison dramas available on Netflix, HBO GO, Amazon, and elsewhere. Compare the ways characters are introduced. How do the shows differ in their portrayals of women and men? Does the difference in tone affect the kinds of stories that are told?
- On the Writers Guild of America website, find the guidelines for new media in the 2014 Minimum Basic Agreement (MBA). How do provisions in new media differ from conventional agreements?

CHAPTER TWO

THE OLD WORLD

JUST BECAUSE YOU LEAVE A PLACE doesn't mean it isn't there.

Traditional networks continue to build citadels, or to erode like sand castles, depending on whom you ask. Despite the excitement of the "new" — new platforms, new technologies, new audiences, new kinds of programming, new ways of financing television — most people watch the same free broadcasting stations as they did in the 20th century. And those mainstream audiences tend to watch similar sorts of shows — plots that "close" (complete their episodic stories), offering comfort within their half-hour or hour time slots, and are viewed once a week on the network schedule.

For example, the number one scripted series in 2014 was *NCIS* on CBS network, a military-legal procedural that attracts almost 20 million viewers in its hour each week. Overall, each of the four legacy networks — ABC, CBS, NBC, Fox — averages nearly 10 million viewers per prime-time hour. That means 30 to 40 million people are watching the four traditional outlets each hour of prime time every day. That's a whole lot of people.

In comparison, the top cable show, *The Walking Dead*, gets around 12 million views in its first run on AMC (a little over half of NCIS). But even award-winning cable shows like *Mad Men* tend to be in the 2 to 3 million range when first aired. (Delayed viewing adds to everyone's numbers, of course.)

Now look at web series. For the moment, let's set aside Netflix shows that are in a premium subscription category of their own, and numbers are not available. An average scripted web series (meaning a fully written,

THE OLD WORL
FOX
CBS
NBC
ABC

full-length original show, not cat videos) may count itself a blockbuster if it has a million viewers, and "successes" on YouTube are in the hundreds of thousands; in fact many have fan bases of just a few thousand.

As a snapshot, compare 10 million viewers on a broadcast hour to 2 million on a cable hour to 200,000 on a non-premium web series. Those proportions are changing fast, and certain YouTube shows claim numbers in the millions for short funny videos if they go viral. But be wary. As excitement rises when new islands appear on the horizon, keep perspective on the magnitude of the continent receding behind you.

While we're talking numbers, here's a stunner: 30% of all people watching anything in prime time are watching it on Netflix. I was told that by a researcher at Google/YouTube, who had nothing to gain from these statistics. Later I checked it at a network that agreed. Netflix doesn't release statistics, so it remains more like a rumor. But, if accurate, the second part of the research is even more striking: many of those people watching Netflix instead of broadcast stations are actually watching broadcast shows. Old ones. Sometimes very old and long off the air.

Whether they're watched on Netflix or Hulu or DirecTV or Amazon or iTunes or Roku or somewhere else, interest continues in long-departed series. The persistence of these reruns brings us to a completely current reality: all eras are one on television; we inhabit an eternal *now*.

That's not to say television is static. Change is upon us, and with the ascent of quality original content on premium cable and online, traditional broadcast networks seem to have lost their mojo among creators and critics, if not the middle-of-the-road audience. The networks know it, and they're defensive.

In my interviews for this book I spoke with executives in both old and new media. Among network leaders, two comments exemplify the problem. Soon after the 2013 Emmys, in which no broadcast network won a major award, a Senior VP complained to me, "I don't know why we don't win anything. We're as good as anyone else." That was followed a few sen-

AMC's zombie drama *The Walking Dead* outperformed every scripted show on television this season in the advertiser-coveted 18- to 49-year old demographic.

tences later with "If we'd tried to make *Breaking Bad* here, we'd all have been fired." Apparently, he didn't notice the connection.

Every year in May, in a ritual called the "upfronts," all the networks go to New York to compete for the next season's advertising dollars. "There's an air of urgency for the suits at the legacy networks," the *L.A. Times* reported in 2013. "They've been rocked by an ominous first: a basic cable program — AMC's zombie drama *The Walking Dead* — outperformed every scripted show on television this season in the advertiser-coveted 18- to 49-year old demographic. And zombies are the least of it. Competition is closing in from every corner and on every device. DVRs are frustrating advertisers by allowing viewers to skip ads. Netflix, Amazon, and a host of online web services are producing original fare."

The networks are losing because "they don't have the tolerance for risk," according to Kevin Aratari, Managing Director of the ad firm mOcean. "They can't put a million dollars or more on an episode and have a show flop." Interviewed at the upfronts, Aratari summarized, "It's like the Wild West a bit right now. And no one has nailed it down."

To understand what all this might mean to you as a writer-creator, you first need to know:

HOW NETWORK SHOWS WORK

If you want to write for television — old, new, or anything in between — you first need to be able to write. Like any other profession, skills and experience are essential to launch or advance a career. With the proliferation of film schools, screenwriting classes, and development workshops, most people bring well-honed portfolios to the table. That's especially true at the traditional networks, where most of the jobs still are.

Don't be fooled. The fantasy of breaking into "Hollywood" on luck, charm, and an idea is just that — a fantasy — even in this era of expanding opportunity. First learn your craft.

Probably you've already read my earlier book *Writing the TV Drama Series, Third Edition* (2011). That's the essential companion to this one. In it, I walk you through every step of the process. Chapter Two of that book tells how shows get on TV and details two years of TV seasons. The network system is explained on pages 45–77. Chapters Three and Four describe exactly how to craft a professional episode from pitch through outline and first and second drafts. This would be a good time to review those chapters so you'll have a context for what is changing.

Continuing with what's new, I spoke with Trey Callaway, Executive Producer on NBC's successful series *Revolution.* Here are his candid answers and his advice.

TREY CALLAWAY

PAMELA DOUGLAS: Is your process of pitching, developing, or running a show any different from what it was a few years ago?

TREY CALLAWAY: I think it is in a lot of respects. One change is not entirely healthy in that the TV business is borrowing from the feature business in that their source

"Networks are about what's the big franchise-able idea." — *Revolution* producer Trey Callaway

materials become extremely important, in some cases too important. It's not enough to have a great original idea for a series. It's often as important to have source materials behind it — a book, a comic book, a previous television series, "based on a… " It gives networks and studios a comfort level, feeling like they're plugging into an existing track record.

There are certain cases when I'll have an original idea that I'll then reverse-engineer to a certain extent and go find source materials that can semi-support the idea. I can make my whole pitch and then throw the book down on the table and say oh, by the way, here's this historical figure's biography that functions as a bible for eleven seasons of the series.

Along with that, attachments have become more important, like in the feature business. That's all reflective of working for the same five or six media conglomerates, so the strategies those companies use start to mirror each other. It becomes important that you're connected with this or that producer or that piece of talent who has an existing deal. Considering that TV is, and continues to be, a writer's medium, there are a lot of other people you have to pull onto your bandwagon with you, elements you have to stack in order to beat the increasing odds.

And there's another new wrinkle, though not necessarily a healthy one. Because networks and studios are about what's the big franchise-able idea, what's going to justify our costs and run twelve seasons, because they're so focused on that, there's an increasing tendency to buy ideas from people who have no previous television experience, whether that's because they've been in features or they're literally baby writers. There are two people working a lot right now in the business: kids that are literally fresh out of USC (in some cases, still students there), and the Oscar-winning heavyweights. The middleman gets closed out. The working-class writer who keeps the guilds alive and the craft alive gets pushed out.

I think it's easier now than it's been in a while for new voices, new talent to rise quickly. It's not necessarily the best thing for them, and they inevitably get partnered with people who are experienced, so there's that job classification available for working writers. With the increased number of venues there's an increased demand for content.

PD: This model that fits the networks with high concept and broad audiences is actually contrary to what's happening online.

TC: These big companies tend to move like slow-moving cruise ships and it takes them a long time to adjust their courses. As attractive as *Game of Thrones* is on HBO, when you compare the viewership of that to the average viewing audience of *NCIS*, it's an entirely different experience, so it's hard to fault the big networks for a "broadcasting" model because they're connecting with tens of millions of people every night.

PD: For talented young people with no credits graduating out of school into today's world, who want to do television, where do they start?

TC: This is another seismic shift in the TV business. I don't think it's healthy but in the last few years I've seen the elimination of the staff writer position. That's tough on kids just beginning their careers.

I understand that if I'm a showrunner because of budget pressures and increasing competition from other shows, staffs are smaller than they used to be. I have X number of dollars to spend on a staff, and as much as I'd love to experiment on new voices and to bring some of my former students up along the ranks, if I only have X dollars to spend it's in my best interest to hire as many high-level proven writers as I can. These are people who have great track records on turning in drafts and know the game so I can hit the ground running and I don't have to teach anybody the TV business. From my own perspective I want to mentor people, but increasingly that's not the case.

It's far more important now for beginners to find writer's assistant positions. They function in a similar way as staff writer positions used to because you're getting into the room and exposed to the process and are able to contribute to the process. You're not being paid or credited as you would be as a staff writer, though. But then where there's a call for volunteers for that freelance episode over Christmas that nobody wants to write, you're in the room. You turn to the people who already are in the room. They may need some hand-holding on their first execution, still they know the voices and the process and that's valuable.

PD: Besides getting on a staff, what about developing? A lot of people may go off-network for their first break.

TC: There are more opportunities off-network, and they'll take more risks. I say tell and sell your story wherever you can find a willing audience.

FRONT DOORS TO THE NETWORKS

In *Writing the TV Drama Series* you'll find a whole chapter on how to break into traditional media. So this is a good time to read Chapter Six from page 227 to 239. Updating that advice, I spoke with Carole Kirschner, a former CBS executive and author of *Hollywood Game Plan*, who also heads the CBS Television Writers Program and runs a consulting service called "Park on the Lot."

CAROLE KIRSCHNER

PAMELA DOUGLAS: What would you tell a young person who came to you, a good writer who asks I want to break into television, what do I do now?

CAROLE KIRSCHNER: First you write incredible material and you make sure it's incredible by having someone in the business read it. Then, if you qualify, you get into one of the network programs. That's the fastest way to get representation.

PD: How do they get into that?

CK: They apply in the spring. For CBS they need an original piece of material such as a pilot, plus a spec episode. NBC and ABC both require specs, and ABC also wants other things. Warners requires a spec and backup material. Also Fox. They need to know you have a body of work, so you wouldn't even apply until you have a whole body of work. To get that body of work people should take classes. It's presumptuous to say 'I've never written anything but I watch television so I should be able to write television.' It's just not true. They should learn how to write and then practice writing.

Another way to go is do everything you can to get a job as a writer's p.a., not a writer's assistant because that's five steps up. Writer's assistant is the entry point; it used to be staff writer, but now it's writer's assistant. Find somebody who knows somebody who knows somebody who knows somebody who will take your application to be a writer's p.a. Sometimes you can do it cold, though, by asking if you can apply — 'May I send my resume?' If they say no, you ask, 'May I call you back in a few weeks?' It always helps to have someone recommend you.

And absolutely enter every writing contest you can. Win the first or second prize, but don't put down that you're a quarterfinalist because no one cares.

PD: I'm hearing a degree of impatience from showrunners. They say we need writers to be skilled by the time they're here so they can hit the ground running.

CK: That's not everybody. There are different kinds of showrunners. Some are willing to take people with talent and bring them up. But there are far smaller writing staffs, so when they hire somebody they do need that person to perform well. Still, I'm hearing we don't look for baby writers to be writing drafts; we just expect them to sit and learn. There's more room for that in cable — the staffs may be smaller but there's more time to make the show, so there's more time to work on the scripts.

I also found practical advice for you from Jennifer Grisanti, an instructor for NBCs "Writers on the Verge" development program. Author of *Change Your Story, Change Your Life*, Grisanti runs a private consultancy.

JENNIFER GRISANTI

PAMELA DOUGLAS: Many of your recent clients have placed pilots. Would you talk about their process? I have a feeling it was close to the traditional methods.

JENNIFER GRISANTI: When clients sell pilots it's a village coming into play. People come to story consultants to learn about how to develop stories in the strongest way possible. It's never an overnight thing, as much as people want to believe that. It's working together to get a script to the best place possible and then utilizing a manager or agent to get it to the network or studio. And then it's a matter of the script deal. Out of the 20 pilots my clients have sold, only two have gone to series. It's just a step toward that process.

PD: Are they selling to traditional networks or where?

JG: 85% traditional network and 15% cable. I haven't had anybody sell a web series.

PD: If a beginner came to you with writing skills but no agent or manager or any connections, what would you advise?

JG: I love when people have had another career and then come to me because they have something to write about. For a new writer it's all about creating a portfolio. It's also about managing expectations. If they imagine they're going to write one pilot and make it I help them understand how our business works. This could be a five-to-ten-year journey before anything happens. A manager once said if you're not going to give it five years, don't give it five minutes.

Being a writer is like being on a roller coaster. When you get that first staff job, that isn't the end. It's the beginning. You may need to learn social skills because you're going to be working in a writers' room with the same people ten hours a day.

I tell writers to plan to have three original scripts in their portfolio and current spec scripts. I believe they should have current spec scripts. I've staffed 15 shows and I've had showrunners who would not read pilots; I also had showrunners who would read pilots but after they read the pilots they wanted to read a spec script to understand if the writer knew how to mimic somebody else's voice. That hasn't gone away. I wouldn't recommend having only original material. You're hurting yourself if someone asks for a spec script and you don't have one.

The writers I work with who have the most success have a number of scripts. They send their submissions to programs and hope they do well in a competition or get into a program and that leads to getting an agent or manager and that leads to staffing.

RUNNING YOUR OWN SHOW

What if you really want to create and run your own show? Be careful what you wish for.

The news for writers who have already been on network staffs is a program run by the Writers Guild of America, West. In 2005 the Showrunner Training Program (STRP) began to teach the next generation of writer-producers how to make the leap to top management. You apply through the Guild and competition for the few spaces each year is stiff. Jeff Melvoin, the program's founder, Emmy-winner for *Northern Exposure* and a veteran of *Remington Steele*, *Hill Street Blues*, *Picket Fences*, and *Alias*, "noticed that the number of scripted programs were expanding, creating an unprecedented demand for showrunners. At the same time opportunities were dwindling for writers to learn on the job through long apprenticeships," according to *Written By* (the WGA magazine).

Melvoin describes the top job as "hiring, firing, handholding, scolding, cheerleading, negotiating, cajoling, firefighting, inspiring, and then repeating all of these things to the point of either exhaustion or cancellation." His advice: "Stop thinking like an employee and begin thinking like a CEO."

John Wells, showrunner on *ER*, *West Wing*, *Shameless*, and *Southland*, cautioned, "a network will be handing you $30 million and telling you to hire people, start in eight weeks, and produce something in seven months."

Undaunted, let's say you're going out with an original pilot and a full head of steam. Well, Yvette Bowser, creator of the Queen Latifah sitcom *Living Single* and many comedy pilots, advised the STRP that odds are against success. "You have to want it but not want it too much. If you're getting 10% of your pilots picked up, you're golden. And you have to realize that."

That's not meant to be discouraging, just real, as you contemplate opportunities in the mainstream. Aron Coleite, whose resume includes *Crossing Jordan*, *Heroes*, and *The River*, told *Written By*: "The reason I wanted to be a television writer is because I love the writers' room. You don't have to sit alone. As a group, you can share the wealth of the torment among friends. That's how you create something, and that's how you create a community of artists.... We're all sort of programmed to want to become showrunners. We all want to have our own shows, yet there's so much more to do than simply crafting the writing and the creative vision."

BACK DOORS TO THE NETWORKS

Nowadays, the ways to get into traditional networks are no longer traditional.

Carole Kirschner observes, "There are lots of 22-year-old agents' assistants who spend their lives going on the web looking for the next new voice. So someone could potentially get 'discovered' by having his or her work online. The way people get representation or find their way in is still writing contests, which have been going on for a long time. But having an online component is what's new."

Some broadcast outlets are creating their own "minor leagues" of new series online. For instance, the CW launched CW Seed as a subsite on CWTV.com, with the tagline "What's Next." "I think this is a kind of a unique thing for a broadcast network to do, to have an incubator to really look at and get feedback from the fans," said Rick Haskins, CW Executive VP of marketing and digital programs. We can test out new talent, test out new ideas, test out new ways for finding exciting new opportunities for advertisers and moving [the successful shows] to the mainstream CW."

Success is counted in new ways too. *The Vampire Diaries* on the CW had around 17 million Facebook "likes" by the end of 2013, compared with around 18 million for *NCIS* and 20 million for *The Walking Dead*. Its fifth-season premiere garnered 278,000 tweets. For the young-skewing CW audience those numbers might mean more than traditional Nielsen ratings, and gives young writers a clue to building buzz for a show of their own.

Can you really tweet or blog your way to a show? For a legacy network, these sources can be seen as ways of keeping up with the times… or acts of desperation. The test is if the blogs and tweets are able to work as storytelling over enough hours. That is, can 140 characters embody enough narrative potential to roll out even one season, even a limited series of eight to 12 episodes? How about a Tumblr blog consisting mostly of hand-drawn musings about being 20-something?

At this writing, NBC has put in development *F*ck! I'm in My Twenties*, as a half-hour comedy series based on Emma Koenig's Tumblr blog about just that. Here's a sample of one of Koenig's entries, hand-written: "When anything VERY GOOD happens to me, I can only enjoy it for so long before I think: COUNTDOWN TO PEOPLE RESENTING ME: 5!4!3!2!1!"

Okay, students, here's your assignment: From that raw material find the inciting moment that will drive action in the pilot. Delineate the antagonist and his or her goals and internal conflict. Develop the "worst case" break in the story that will culminate the rising conflict. Create a twist in the resolution of the pilot that leverages the next episodes. Then suggest how those potentials play out over an arc of a season with emphasis on arcs for supporting cast in addition to the protagonist. Then, after all that is done, demonstrate opportunities for humor and clarify the kind of humor (satire, farce, situational, and so forth) that completes this as a comedy series. Can you describe hilarious moments or write jokes drawn from this premise?

No doubt NBC is on top of all that and more by giving Koenig experienced co-writers and top executive producers. Since Koenig herself is not going to run the show, or write it, that makes me wonder what it is they bought, and whether they were really after the imprint of someone in a desired demographic as opposed to actual television writing.

Nor is that the only Tumblr blog to get a TV adaptation. Earlier, Lauren Bachelis' *Hollywood Assistants* blog was set up as a comedy at CBS. The show titled *20-Nothings* has a similar profile of attaching experienced talent to run it. And the same question arises: Apart from the sourcing, how much is this kind of deal actually development from a nontraditional venue, and how much is it a very traditional development from an idea, similar to the way shows have been developed from pitches for decades?

Are tweets and blogs just a new form of pitching to traditional networks? And do they work?

No, according to Justin Halpern, creator of the Twitter feed *Shit My Dad Says*. Halpern's tweets got so many fans that he expanded his dad's irascible quotations into short stories that he collected into a book. And then CBS came calling. The network picked up the tweets and book to make into a standard multicam sitcom. That's when everything fell apart.

Halpern explained to *Splitsider* (an online site), "In this case, my dad is a guy who is not trying to be funny, which is why I think the Twitter feed and my book were so successful. He's not a guy who's 'jokey.' In multicam, you tend to play to the joke, it's more setup/punchline, just by nature of shooting in front of a live audience, and that kind of cuts the nuts off my dad as a character. So even when we shot the pilot, I thought, 'fuuuuuuuuck. This is not my book. This is not working for this character.'"

Halpern also claims he felt silenced by the network, who didn't think audiences would want to watch a wacky older guy talking about atheism or swearing. "I realized this wasn't my father after I got the Standards and Practices notes when we turned in the first script and we couldn't say ANY of the words my father uses, nor discuss any of the things my dad discusses."

His final assessment to *Splitsider*: "The network gets scared because they invested a ton of money into the show. And when they freak out, the notes get larger and suddenly you have 12 people saying, 'Why is that plumber walking through the front door?' and you're like 'Fuck I don't know, he's the plumber. I guess this needs a page one rewrite?'"

WHAT CAN THE NETWORKS DO?

Okay, reality check. What if Twitter is not really "all that"? Or webisodes either.

Remember the 30 to 40 million people watching the networks? They're still watching. And the numbers seem to be growing now that networks have quit defending themselves against DVR (digital video recorders — delayed viewing on other platforms) and learned to embrace the audiences who may not sit down at the same time and even those who skip the commercials.

For example, a week after its premiere on NBC, *The Blacklist* had been seen by around 18 million viewers, once the 6 million or so who watched later were counted. Where are all those people watching? Well, not on the same network that first aired the show because it isn't there. Broadcasters have made deals with online services like Hulu and Amazon, where audiences now find network shows. But, hey, they find them.

ABC was ahead of the game in 2005 when they reached an agreement with Apple Inc. to sell Disney's TV shows through the tech giant's iTunes store. The liaison came just a few months before Disney added Apple chief Steve Jobs to its board. Later that year, ABC became the first network to offer its programs to viewers on the Internet.

So instead of competing, broadcasters are trying to figure out how to exploit the digital platforms without losing those viewers from their own channels. It's tricky, but possible.

For example, catch-up viewing of shows people have missed can drive people back to the network that originally televised the show. Alternately, a big opening on a network can be engineered as an "event" to drive audience to continue the series on a smaller outlet (like a cable station or online) owned or licensed by the network.

Another approach is for the legacy networks to proudly own their mainstream identities. Maybe the time is over for them to be the places for innovation, niche programs, and passionate fans. Instead, they can become more like today's movie theaters that attract crowds to a few franchise-driven blockbuster events while ceding lower budget character-driven stories to spaces that don't need so much spectacle.

Or maybe the networks will keep fighting to be more like the cable channels. For example, *Extant*, executive produced by Steven Spielberg and starring Halle Berry ventured into premium quality on CBS in the summer of 2014.

Les Moonves, Chief Executive of CBS Corp., says he plans to imitate cable and offer shortened seasons where the creative quality is easier to maintain. Compare the 22- or 24-episode season at a network with the 12 episodes per year that are normal on Showtime or AMC or HBO. From a writer's viewpoint the shorter season allows breathing room to think and rewrite. That's good news for you.

Or maybe CBS doesn't have to do anything different because its profits are rising just fine. Commenting on the network's profits, Moonves said, "Success was led by our content businesses, which continue to prove that this is a golden age for those who have the best programming." And, in fact, huge numbers of people are watching television of all kinds.

So, the Old World traditional networks might remain pretty much as they are for quite a while. Of course, they are no longer the only places for writers to work, and if we quit expecting them to be what they aren't, maybe we could just accept them as one more option in a universe of possibilities.

INTERACT WITH CHAPTER TWO

- Using the tweet from *F*ck! I'm in My Twenties* quoted in Chapter Two, take the challenge presented and create a way to expand the tweet into a series.
- In the book *Writing the TV Drama Series*, read the section on procedurals (pages 145–154). Find a current-day subject that involves clue-driven stories that can "close" in an hour. Use the principles of procedural writing to form your show in a way that could fit the legacy networks.
- *The Big Bang Theory* was the top-rated network comedy in 2014. Compare its geek characters to the 2014 HBO comedy *Silicon Valley*. How do interpretations of this subject differ?
- Still considering computer- and geek-centric stories, how would you do an original series about characters immersed in this world? How can women and girls be involved in these male social groups?

CHAPTER THREE

BETWEEN WORLDS— CABLE TV

IMAGINE YOU'VE LEFT YOUR HOME PLANET — and not yet arrived at your new world. Between here and there are asteroids in space. That's where cable television resides, between two worlds.

Each of these midway asteroids is unique. They range from luxury resorts to art enclaves, schools, animal sanctuaries, garbage dumps, crisis intervention centers, brothels, open marketplaces rife with swindlers, to theme parks for fantasy adventures. Unlike the Old World where traditional television networks tend to be staunchly similar, cable networks are the prodigal colonies that broke away.

Cable can be divided into basic and premium channels. Simply, basic channels are bundled with whatever system provides your general television service (possibly also your Internet and phone). You probably don't subscribe specifically to CNN, for example; it's in the overall package. Basic cable shows are advertiser-supported (sponsored) with commercial breaks just like traditional network shows. Entertainment channels such as FX, AMC, TNT, Comedy Central, E!, Lifetime, Syfy, and many more are "basic," even though the top tier offers "premium" quality content.

Subscription channels are premium cable, and do not have ads. Removing commercials has an impact on storytelling: it opens new ways to form your scripts. Without the need to insert advertising at predetermined intervals, the four-, five-, or six-act structure, familiar in traditional

Between Worlds
Yahoo
Hulu
CNN
FX
COMEDY CENTRAL
HBO
AMC
Cinemax
SHOWTIME
Starz
History
Telemundo

television and basic cable, becomes flexible. So writing without essential cliff-hangers at each act break allows the recurrent jeopardy to the main cast to be less urgent, or at least less predictable. (See Chapter Three in *Writing the TV Drama Series* for a full discussion of act structures.) In the United States, premium/subscription cable includes Showtime, Starz, Cinemax, and HBO, though "pay television" is different in other countries.

It's not really that simple, though. A classy joint like AMC benefits from being chosen by viewers who buy basic cable packages and opt to include the AMC network (AMC, IFC, Sundance). In other words, though viewers don't directly subscribe to AMC, in the same sense as subscribing specifically to HBO, viewers do exert leverage on services to carry that network because people value it, and AMC can negotiate participation in pricing.

Further blurring the lines, many cable channels now have online deals or online components. Web-only producers make the case that cable delivery will soon disappear, merging into online distribution. Whether that affects screenwriting and the quality of shows remains to be seen. For now, using AMC as an example again, viewers can access *Breaking Bad* on Netflix, which streams it without ads. (Incidentally don't feel bad for watching AMC on Netflix; Charles Collier of AMC and Ted Sarandos of Netflix get along fine — this is a good business arrangement for all concerned.) So some categories aren't what they used to be now that everything is everywhere.

Still, we can talk about how your opportunities vary with the terrain.

BASIC CABLE CHANNELS

FX

Nick Grad, Executive VP of Original Programming at FX, said his greatest challenge is finding a show that will cut through the increasingly crowded marketplace. "Sometimes you feel like you have to light your hair on fire just to get people to pay attention to you," he told *Broadcasting & Cable* online magazine. "The show has to be great; good does not cut it."

As an offshoot of Fox, FX has staked its ground in unflinching macho dramas and surprisingly honest comedies. That's part of branding — the way channels plant flags for their products so they are recognizable — and it's not new. Former FX Entertainment President Kevin Reilly reported that writing submissions to FX increased tenfold in the 15 months after *The Shield*'s premiere in 2002 (the show ran to 2008). That meant that inside the industry, writers started looking to FX as a place to sell certain kinds of stories. And it was. They followed *The Shield* with similarly edgy dramas including *Justified, Sons of Anarchy*, *The Americans*, and *American Horror Story*, among others. In comedy, *It's Always Sunny in Philadelphia* was an early effort, followed by the acclaimed *Louie* by Louis C.K.

So it was not surprising when Guillermo del Toro (*Hellboy, Pan's Labyrinth, Pacific Rim*) joined other refugees from feature films and created a 2014 series for FX. Based on *The Strain*, a trilogy of books he cowrote about the outbreak of a vampire virus, he brought his cinematic vision to basic cable. Though del Toro is not the showrunner — that is experienced television producer Carlton Cuse who ran *Lost* (with Damon Lindelof) — del Toro stayed involved, and this is typical of the innovations in the top tier of basic cable.

If you think about pitching an original show or working on one, first understand the brand and don't confuse a cable channel's attitude with those of its parent. Fox — the broadcast network — runs series watched mostly by teen girls and young women, often light romances, predictable procedurals, or spooky fantasies that don't rattle the expectations of mainstream viewers. Among Fox network series stars you'll recognize models for beauty products who appear on the covers of women's magazines.

In contrast, FX has the tattooed guys on motorbikes that the girls on Fox wouldn't dare date.

AMC

AMC is the basic cable powerhouse that beat out traditional networks and most other channels to win Emmys for Best Drama Series (not to mention all the writing and other awards) for *Mad Men* and then *Breaking Bad.* And at the same time, this little outlet that used to be known only for movie reruns amassed more viewers in its time period for *The Walking Dead* than any traditional network. A few years ago, I asked AMC President Charlie Collier how they did it all in less than a decade.

CHARLIE COLLIER

CHARLIE COLLIER: If you look at the way we launched *Mad Men*, it illustrates our strategy of originals complementing our movies, and is a great example of our mission in action. *Mad Men*'s lead-in was *GoodFellas*, one of my favorite films. Loosely speaking, it's about a group of men who think they're above the rules. It's a film that has themes that crossed over beautifully into its lead-out, *Mad Men*, also a story about a group of men to whom the rules do not apply; it's cinematic and it's of the highest television quality in every way.

With *Mad Men*, we had success with a period piece. As they say, 'imitation is the sincerest form of television' and, as such, many a period piece hit Development's desks soon after the series premiered — stories of flappers and Motown and the '70s. But we didn't want to become the period piece network. We were looking for a modern-day story that had some of the qualities of the films we curate.

Not unlike *Mad Men*, *Breaking Bad* was led by an 'auteur,' Vince Gilligan. Vince delivered a story that was so wonderful in its description of Walter White's transformation, nuanced in every way; and we all fell in love with the script.

These serialized dramas have each been passion projects led by writers with clear and strong visions. It's a joy to nurture them. I appreciate their talents, their vision, and their true craft in building the character and context. I think anyone who gets into the business, and who doesn't have a healthy appreciation for the content and the brilliant people who create the best of it, is in the wrong business. It's certainly a point of distinction for AMC, how deeply into the organization the creative is valued, with so many of us being true fans of the content, from the top of the organization on down.

One early goal we set — and it remains our goal today at AMC — is to create an environment where the best in the business will bring us their passion projects because they believe AMC will nurture them differently, and better, than anywhere else.

There's a character-development emphasis in the stories that we have an appreciation for. If you speak with Matt Weiner and others who have inspired us, they're telling stories where character and character-based drama comes first. And as with the 'characters' you love in real life, it takes some time to understand who people really are. *Mad Men* and *Breaking Bad* each do wonderfully well with character, sharing the little things that make the characters' stories so much more than what you could ever learn about them in, for example, a typical crime procedural that wraps up in an hour.

Matt Weiner has said there's drama in a phone ringing and no one picking it up. You learn from these brilliant writers that life and storytelling and character development is in the details. And we're willing to invest in these writers because we love the way they tell patient stories and nurture those details.

We set out to create a level of distinction for the AMC brand. The vision is and was to create 'premium television on basic cable' and to do that, my amazing team sought and delivered storytelling that at times has a cadence to it that is very different from what you might find elsewhere."

An International Perspective on AMC

As I've traveled the globe speaking with groups of professional writers in several countries, I discovered everyone knows the AMC shows. In fact I've never spoken to an audience where people did not respond to mention of Don Draper. But none of these countries could actually receive AMC. Equally puzzling was why global audiences were interested in such a sliver of Americana as Madison Avenue advertising in the 1950s and '60s, when their own nations were experiencing very different histories. My only explanation is that depth of character transcends regions. Or maybe the drive to learn how to write well can overcome any barrier. Whatever the reason, these dedicated writers somehow found the shows via the web, satellite transmissions, or DVDs, and the bootleg business in illegal AMC properties seemed to be flourishing everywhere I visited.

Recently, AMC Networks acquired Liberty Global's Chellomedia for more than a billion dollars to increase its *legal* international presence. Chellomedia has around 70 channels in about 140 countries. That gives AMC almost 400 million homes for its products in Europe and Latin America. This global outreach is yet another sign of the times for cable.

IFC

More than twenty years ago, an undergraduate named Dan Pasternak sat in one of my beginning screenwriting classes at USC, so long ago that students made 16mm indie films (now the School of Cinematic Arts does a whole lot more, especially in television and interactive games). We were both beginners — he the postadolescent stand-up comedian learning how to write, and me learning how to teach the craft while I was a new writer on network series.

I didn't remember Dan. As the VP of Development at IFC (Independent Film Channel), which is part of the AMC network, he responded to my email asking for an interview saying he remembered me. We planned to meet when he was in Los Angeles on business, since IFC is based in New York. Maybe I would recognize him then. But the gray-haired man across from me in a restaurant was far beyond the kid in school. And what he'd made of his life was even further beyond what either of us thought might come to exist in the industry. After all, a basic cable channel devoted to sophisticated comedy would have been impossible in the 20th century.

Talking with Dan opened a window into the process of creating a new channel's identity from scratch. I'll let him tell you his creative journey.

DAN PASTERNACK

DAN PASTERNACK: When I thought about becoming a producer or a creative executive, I realized what writers needed was someone who was creatively friendly that could be a partner, a facilitator for the process. I knew about the form that shows and storytelling needed to take. And as I was learning about the business of the business, I could see this process from several different angles. I got my first development job when I was 25-26. I've enjoyed this role of being a guy you can bring an idea to, who can help give it shape and definition and bring it to life.

I spent the first seven or eight years doing what I do mostly within the broadcast world. But that process didn't suit me. It seemed broken. It felt fear-based, desperate. The budgets were bigger, the stakes were higher, and there were usually way too many cooks in the kitchen. Woody Allen described his mother's process of making chicken as running it through the de-flavorizing machine. That's kind of how I felt about working in network television.

Bill Cosby said, "If you try to be everything to everyone you'll be nothing to nobody."

What I saw at IFC was an opportunity. What was about to happen at IFC was similar to what had happened at AMC. IFC was the Independent Film Channel, and being just a movie channel in the age of Netflix was not a great business to try and stay in. If you were going to be a network, and they already had a business plan to become an ad-supported network, the way to make your network a must-add for any cable or satellite provider is to have something no one else has. That's where original programming comes in.

What I brought to my position was this philosophy of how to be distinctive, how to differentiate us from everyone else. I knew what the challenges would be at IFC because we wouldn't have a lot of the resources that the competitors have. You can't be Estonia and win the arms race. So you then have to find the unconquered territory and go out and claim it.

If you look across the spectrum of who is doing scripted comedy on cable, HBO and Showtime's half hour felt more like dramedies. The competition, apart from those premium channels, then would be Adult Swim, FX, and Comedy Central. Adult Swim came up with a distinctive aesthetic and voice — more absurdist and surrealistic. Everything at Adult Swim felt like an Adult Swim show. So they carved out a really distinctive niche.

Still I knew there were a lot of content creators who had no place to go with what they were doing. But I felt that so-called 'alternative comedy' wasn't an alternative anymore. It was kind of like what I saw in the '80s and '90s with so-called "indie rock." When U2 became the biggest band in the world you couldn't really call them an alternative rock band anymore. I saw talent coming from the alternative comedy world having more mainstream success but there still seemed to be no specific home for them on television.

When I thought of the comedies IFC had acquired in the past, like *Arrested Development* or *Monty Python*, I asked myself what do they have in common: they're silly and smart. That's our brand — silly and smart. Our tag line is "Always On, Slightly Off."

I said let's not try to be Comedy Central. Let's not be Adult Swim. Let's program content that feels uniquely like IFC. So one of the very first shows I helped to develop was *Portlandia.* And fortunately it clicked enough to become brand-defining. It doesn't belong anywhere else. Sketch comedy has evolved in the age of the digital short. Essentially each episode of *Portlandia* is eight little movies. But it's really one unified perspective, voice, look, and feel. And there's always one more expansive piece that's broken into kind of a three-act play that has a narrative that pulls through the whole episode. You can sample the show in broken up pieces but the real reward is to watch the whole half hour. The deal with most sketch shows is that you can drop in and out and watch the best of the pieces online. But we were really thoughtful about wanting it to be a show where the audience would want to see the whole half hour of *Portlandia* as it was crafted, as it was intended to be seen. As a TV show. Not just a random collection of shorts. And I think the runner — that linear narrative with a three-act structure inside each episode — was key to helping to make the half hour a cohesive, satisfying viewing experience.

IFC is a cable channel. We are in the business of making longer form shows. That's not to say sketch shows can't be broken into pieces or people can't binge-watch clips. But our business is to make half-hour comedy TV series that perform on the channel. It's great that the shows do well on digital platforms and internationally. But we're focused on doing half-hour comedy series that will be sticky enough that people will show up here to watch the half hours. *Portlandia* was carefully engineered in that way and yet it still feels totally authentic and hand-crafted. Which it is.

Ultimately your shows have to do the heavy lifting. Your shows have to be the ambassadors for the network. And my goal is for us to get enough hit shows so people think of us as a destination.

NICHE CABLE

In a way, all cable television is "niche." Compared to the big broadcast networks, cable channels are specialists, though not as narrowly targeted as web series. On the Internet where "real estate" is cheap or free, anyone can make a series and post it no matter how few people are likely to follow. Cable shows cost to produce and require some sort of backing, usually from advertisers, so even niche-specific channels need enough viewers. But "enough" has become a shrinking bubble.

In *The Television Will Be Revolutionized*, Professor Amanda Lotz analyzed, "… Channels for distinctive audiences — MTV's adolescents, Univision's Spanish speakers, Lifetime's traditional women — are not nearly as exclusive as programming at the extremes, but they also raise the question of how to understand the contribution of exceptional niche shows relative to the mass hits that remain. While many tell stories about specific groups of people, they were never meant to reach only people who look like those on the screen.

"After years of living amidst so much niche media... audiences that could find themselves amply represented on some shows grew uncertain of those that did not feature people who looked like them or whom they might emulate. This situation has fueled a retreat of the audience into enclaves of self-interest, where, despite the medium's enhanced commercial ability to tell a broader range of stories, few of us allow those different from ourselves into our television world."

Case in point: BET (Black Entertainment Television), a thriving channel watched by many African Americans, believes it has basic cable's number one sitcom, *Real Husbands of Hollywood*. Probably you never heard of it if you're not in the select demographic, but in 2013 (when it debuted), it attracted a larger share of adults 18 to 49 than any other original cable comedy. Its finale drew 2.2 million viewers — not a big number for broadcast networks, but impressive on basic cable. You might assume publications like *Entertainment Weekly* would cover it, but the show's only notice was in *Ebony*.

Real Husbands of Hollywood satirizes "reality" shows like *Real Housewives*, but it also satirizes Hollywood and how black people stay afloat. According to the Balder & Dash page on rogerebert.com, it's a "painfully accurate vision of contemporary black Hollywood. It gives black performers a place to show just how much of a cruel, lonely, dog-eat-dog world working in Tinseltown can be. The fact that most of these men's spouses are more successful than they are makes things more frustrating for them."

Chris Rock once said, "You can make a million black people laugh, but one white man will make you rich."

Balder & Dash conclude: "*Real Husbands of Hollywood* has already proven it can make people laugh on a weekly basis. Unfortunately, both the show and the people on it still need important white folk to co-sign for them."

Now multiply that sentiment times every ethnic, cultural, lifestyle, and social group. All those groups have homes on basic cable that range from successful multinational Spanish language entertainment conglomerates like Univision and Telemundo to tiny outlets like Saigon Entertainment TV that does Vietnamese programming.

Basic cable is hundreds of separate cable channels like islands floating in space, each enclosed by its own gravity well, never touching, or even noticed by the others.

GENRE

Fantasy adventure propelled by heroic action has become the bulwark of blockbuster movies. Where spectacle meets technology on large screens in dark theaters, often in 3D, crowds experience vast battles, superhuman feats, extraordinary creatures, and amazing locations. That's a good fit for movies. Games too, as interactive animation is increasingly realistic and both the visuals and music are comparable to films. Off-screen, graphic novels imply many of these same cinematic qualities.

Does the fantasy action/sci-fi genre work as well on television? Yes, it works, but differently. If spectacles are where movies excel, what does television do well?

Let's recall what television does best on any of its platforms: character, intimacy, relationships, ideas — stories that touch viewers who are watching alone or with people who are close, often at home, stories that connect to contemporary experiences and issues that matter because viewers are invested in the characters. That's true no matter what kind of screen you're watching.

Genre shows had been successful on television even before *Twilight Zone* in 1959, but that show became a model, using a limited cast to explore abstract ideas that resonated with its audience. When *Star Trek* came along — both the 1960s original and the 1990s *Next Generation* — the tradition of science fiction anthologies was amplified to an actual series in the form of a family drama that asked questions like what is life, and when does an android have human rights? Though viewers were prompted to imagine off-screen space encounters, both shows had limited locations and casts and concentrated more on relationships and ideas than action.

What about *Game of Thrones*, you ask? Surely that has an immense canvas, shot in multiple climate zones inhabited by seven distinct "kingdoms," and there are lots of battles. But wait a minute. Are there really lots of battles like in *Lord of the Rings*? Think about it. What's actually on screen in *Game of Thrones*? People, right? Characters, often in intimate situations. Relationships within families. Women and men struggling desperately to have power over their personal lives against people with competing personal goals: the essence of dramatic conflict. That HBO foray into genre storytelling may seem superficially to be like fantasy action movies, but it absolutely is television.

In the past decade the fount of genre shows on basic cable has been Syfy Channel. Once upon a time it was Sci Fi, for science fiction, but it gave up such aspirations and seems to have rebranded itself as the place for kitschy monsters. *Sharknado*. Need I say more? Obviously-fake sharks rain from the sky and chomp on the screeching, pretty cast. Right. That was preceded by *Mansquito*. And *Piranhaconda*. Of course, those are TV movies, but they establish the context for Syfy series.

Oddly, Syfy Channel was also the home of one of the most daring and insightful political allegories of the 21st century: *Battlestar Galactica*. The show (a reimagining of a very different 1970s series with the same title) sounds like pure genre, and a summary might feed that misconception — a battle for survival between machines and humans in a distant time in distant space. What made it great was the writing that conveyed the depth of the Cylon characters as much as the humans, and moved the audience to invest emotionally in the expanding awareness within the characters. The metaphoric level, boldly paralleling controversial international politics, was a bonus that elevated good storytelling to a larger meaning. Syfy doesn't do shows like *Battlestar Galactica* anymore, but other channels including premium cable and web series are picking up the gauntlet of science fiction. You *can* write well in this form.

In an article about the *Hunger Games* movies, Andrew Slack, Executive Director of the philanthropic Harry Potter Alliance, commented, "Fantasy is not an escape from our world but an invitation to go deeper into it."

For new writers, plenty of opportunity is out there. Genre can be a way to break in to a career, partly because many genre series aim for thrills that are not always balanced by nuance or complex layers of character, making the storytelling process somewhat easier. Basic cable has opportunities in this area on smaller channels as well as on Syfy, and so do some online networks and youth-skewing broadcast shows. Marvel's initiative into parallel series based on their comics is a beachhead for genre fantasy — but it's on Netflix, and we'll look into that in the section on Netflix.

Regardless of platform, your challenge is to go beyond the expectations.

PREMIUM CABLE

In the golden age of television, premium cable has the gold mines. HBO in particular redefined screen literature by elevating honest, insightful portrayals of human beings. That happened because executives let the writers do it. The cause is that clear.

Premium channels are supported by viewer subscriptions rather than advertising, so that's another source of the freedom to create. And the enthusiasm from fans and reviewers encouraged the evolution along. Other premium channels doing interesting work are Starz, Showtime, and Cinemax. In each case they took chances on material never before on television (or movies), and they promise to keep pushing boundaries in the future.

STARZ, SHOWTIME, AND CINEMAX

Even with all the gore and sex in *Spartacus*, Starz avoided having that multi-year serial sink into porn by emphasizing the intensity of the characters and their deeply held goals. Once you get past the slo-mo flying blood and all the naked people, you might appreciate how *Spartacus* used a fictional ancient Rome to explore class struggle, especially the way society divided between slaves and aristocrats, and the maneuvers for power among those of inherited wealth. No one compares it to the buttoned-up *Downton Abbey*, but think about it.

Having moved the bar for visceral cinema, Starz became a contender in premium television with *Outlander*, based on beloved novels by Diana Gabaldon, and brought to television by Ron Moore of *Battlestar Galactica*. From its pilot on, critical acclaim came from depth of character for the female lead and the intense history of eighteenth-century Scotland. All that pushed this show and Starz beyond its niche in 2014.

Meanwhile, Showtime — home of award-winning *Homeland* — opened the doors to quality dramedies with *Nurse Jackie*, *Weeds*, and *The Big C*. Of course, half-hour dramatic comedies (or comedic dramas) that deliver uncomfortable laughs that come from recognition of truth — the opposite of laugh-track sitcoms — date back to *M*A*S*H* in the 1970s. And Showtime also expanded the "dramedy" field into hour-long "comedy" in *Shameless*. In all these cases, they knew advertiser-based networks couldn't have made shows about drugs, cancer, and alcoholic parents; but without ads they could. From the start, Showtime's intention was to break the mold.

Remember *Dexter*, the lovable serial killer? In the early years of that show, I spoke with Melissa Rosenberg when she was running the writers' room. She rose to executive-produce *Dexter*, and then became the most financially successful woman screenwriter in history with her three *Twilight* movies. Then she returned to produce and write television, where she is currently part of the Marvel-Netflix creative team. But back in 2007 she shared insights with me about working on *Dexter* that still apply to working on current shows:

Melissa Rosenberg

"One of Showtime's requests of us was to not have a formula. It was funny coming out of network television, used to being on shows and trying to find their formula, then to go on to a show where you don't have to do that.

"Our very first conversations are the season arc. We track where we want to go. Then we start breaking it down until we get to the individual episode. Showtime said the objective was really not to be network television. They wanted serialized episodes."

HBO

Still, the template for premium television is HBO. *The Economist* (a British publication) wrote that HBO "has lavished good, smart product on its viewers, and in the process raised the entire industry's creative game. In the late 1990s HBO pioneered an intelligent, patient style of storytelling that gloried in loose ends and morally ambiguous characters, a style *The Sopranos* came to epitomize.

"Even by television's standards HBO offers unusual creative freedom. Alan Ball, who won an Oscar for writing *American Beauty* before joining HBO to create *Six Feet Under*, contrasts HBO with the 'gulag' of broadcast television. He remembers flurries of notes from network executives that squeezed the original ideas out of his scripts. At HBO the notes are fewer and actually helpful."

David Simon, creator of *The Wire*, had a similar writing experience at HBO. He told Alan Sepinwall in *The Revolution Was Televised*: "My rhythms are prose rhythms to an extent. In the beginning the one thing prose could do that TV couldn't do was tell a sophisticated, complicated story. Television couldn't do that because they needed the episodes to stand alone."

Simon discovered that as he wrote *The Wire* over its five years, people told him the show was getting better. Simon responded, "It's not that the episodes were getting better, but it's a cumulative effect.... With *The Wire*, the whole is far greater than the sum of its parts. It isn't designed like any TV show before it, not even the other early successes of this new golden age. It isn't designed to be broken apart into bits, some parts elevated over others or consumed separately."

That history from *Oz* through *The Sopranos* and *The Wire* is a blessing and a curse to HBO now. They're always creating new shows, but they also need to be *perceived* as current. So they threw a party in Silicon Valley for the season premiere of *Game of Thrones*. "Welcome to the new HBO," said Will Richmond, a cable executive and publisher of VideoNuze.com. "Two or three years ago, you wouldn't have seen this mentality from HBO. But the network is trying to be much more tech forward and immerse itself in the tech community."

HBO credits Apple, Amazon, Google, and Microsoft with helping boost the popularity of HBO GO, the online streaming service that makes their series available to anyone who subscribes to the channel. "With TV, it's not just about having a great piece of programming now. It's about delivering that programming on whatever device people want to watch it on, whenever they want to watch it," HBO Chief Operating Officer Eric Kessler said. Clearly, HBO is keeping its eye on the future as Internet and mobile technologies reshape how people watch TV.

On the ground, where shows are actually created, that tech future feels less relevant. Michael Lombardo, HBO's President of Programming, told the *Los Angeles Times Magazine*, "The whole level of excellence in television has risen, and I say 'Hats off!' Do my competitive instincts kick in sometimes? And do I want my show to win an award over someone else's? Sure. But I can't not respect what's going on elsewhere.

"At the same time, the minute we program derivatively or reactively, we've lost sight of who we are and what brought us to this place. The HBO brand, I do believe, still stands for clear, distinct voices. Our role is to listen to — and believe in — a voice and help the creators do their best work. We don't micromanage. If a show requires us to help craft and execute it, then it's probably not the right show for us. We create a place where we trust the creative vision, and where our number one priority is to keep the creators feeling happy, engaged, and supported. That's our job. That's good business for us. We're not going to do it in a different way."

When I interviewed Mike Lombardo, he was excited about then-upcoming 2014 shows *True Detective*, *The Leftovers*, and *Looking*. By the time you read this, they'll be airing, and new projects will be on the way. So rather than deal with specific programming, I'd like to share his overall perspective with you.

MICHAEL LOMBARDO

MICHAEL LOMBARDO: HBO starts with great writing. There's no cheat to it. There's nothing except it starts with the writing, and that has been our mantra from early on. Going forward, it continues to be our mantra in a world where there's a lot of noise — "event television," "branded content." For us, it still comes down to the writing.

Everyone seems to be looking for an event that makes noise. We certainly don't want to be doing what I'd call smaller niche shows but when something comes in front of you that has a compelling story, well told with a unique voice, we still need to bet on it.

When I think about what has worked for us, it's less about event programming than about passion engagement. The only way that happens is — sometimes there are shows that catch on and you scratch your head — but for the most part, what works is something really well told with an authentic voice. This is what we're in. We're not in the business of looking to take a swing on a show thinking this is going to get the most eyeballs in the world. It's just not who we are. Our subscriber is expecting us to do more than that — they can get that on free television. They're expecting singular voices here. They're expecting well-crafted shows here. They're expecting shows that don't cheat, that don't take the easy route, that challenge the viewer. We have to stay true to that.

PAMELA DOUGLAS: What do you think about Netflix? I've heard them called "the new HBO." How do you feel about that?

ML: Imitation is the sincerest form of flattery so it's nice to be treated as the model. We've always lived in a competitive environment with shows emanating from AMC, FX, Showtime, PBS, the broadcast networks, and many others. Netflix is just another entrant putting out programs.

PD: HBO GO is one means of accessing HBO in a new way. Is this something you might look at in the future in terms of no longer doing linear scheduled programming, or getting more into streaming on the Internet?

ML: There are no plans to abandon our linear scheduled programming now. A substantial majority of the population still enjoys scheduled appointment viewing, though that's not true of every show, and people channel surf. At some point we might monetize GO if it's sold along with your HBO package. We're not programming with the streaming model in mind, but I could imagine a day when that happens.

PD: What do you see as the future of cable altogether? HBO pioneered the idea of premium cable way back when, and now we have AMC and other networks. It's become the place for quality, where to look for a model of good writing. But some people say cable as a delivery system is going to bleed away at some point, that it's all going to be online anyway so it doesn't matter if it's called cable or something else. What do you think about that?

ML: I don't know where that tipping point is, whether it's five or ten or fifteen years. People are watching programs online as things are, through a cable box. I think the big challenge for cable viewing on television is (dare I say it) packaging. For a family of four on a moderate income, the pricing for the full panoply of channels is not inexpensive. There's increasing demand from consumers to find an affordable way.

PD: I teach at USC and I have some brilliant MFA students. I'd like to speak to those who are trying to be professional and those who are already new professionals. Everybody thinks it's nuts to propose anything to HBO because you're on such a high mountain.

ML: I have an example of a young executive here who found a script by a young writer named Michael Lannan who was working as a writer's assistant on a show. It needed a lot of work but there was a voice there that was distinctive and so fresh that we brought him in and surrounded him and found a perfect partner for him and the two of them are now running our new series, *Looking*.

The hard part is we don't take unsolicited submissions. How are you going to get in the door? This business is built on agents and managers. If you can't get representation what are you going to do? It's a challenge for us and it's a challenge for a young writer.

We're starting an initiative next year. We sat around talking when *Girls* came on and people were asking why aren't there more African Americans? That's not Lena Dunham's job and we don't believe her show needs to be for every person. We follow the characters and story the creator brings in. But there is a question: Where's the black or Latina *Girls*? The truth is I haven't been pitched that show. Is it because there are no women writing or able to write those scripts? They're not getting in the system and there's no access point for them.

So we're reaching out. We're going to film schools. We're starting a program for young writer-directors and we're going to end up producing some short films each year. It's not that we want the shorts. But that's a way to start developing those people to write something for us or somebody else. We'll bring those people into the system who are not getting access right now. That is a challenge. It's hard to get representation without a job and it's impossible to get in the door without representation.

Aside from the issues of good citizenship and doing the right thing, the proof of the demographics of this country was in the last election. Particularly looking at an under-30 audience, there is an urban experience that is universal now. There is a growing multiracial population and storytelling needs to speak to that audience.

We're not the network that's going to cast the best friend as black and check it off. We start from storytelling. Those storytellers are out there. Maybe we'll need to partner them with somebody; but that's okay, we've done that.

It's a great time for television. It's an exciting time. People are pushing boundaries. There are no limits to the stories you can tell.

What's going on in the movie business both in the volume of movies they make and the kind of movies they make, combined with the realization they can do quality, textured storytelling in television, has resulted in a wholesale migration of artists who never would have thought of writing or directing for the small screen. We have Steven Soderbergh directing ten episodes of *The Knick* that focuses on medicine at the turn of the century, and he's having the experience of his life. Years ago, it wouldn't have entered his mind. That's exciting. But that can't be at the expense of finding new voices. At the end of the day it's the authentic voice we need to keep looking for. That's what differentiates us and that's what makes us who we are.

When we think about what we put into development and what we green-light, what we're thinking about is "Is this excellent?" That's how we got to where we are. Going forward, we have to stay mindful of that; otherwise we're going to be in the fray with everybody else. When you start worrying about servicing an audience instead of supporting a voice you won't have a great show.

THE END OF CABLE TV?

Do you hate your cable provider? You know what I mean — the guys that charge you a bundle to "bundle" stations you don't want. But you subscribe anyway because it's the only way to get the shows you do want, especially the great ones on HBO.

Are we all at the mercy of Comcast, Time Warner, Verizon, and their ilk? Well, an estimated 7.6 million U.S. homes had "cut the cord" by 2014. Then add the millions of "cord-nevers" and you have an increasing number of viewers — especially younger viewers — who have turned to online streaming instead of cable.

All that was already happening when HBO "unleashed the dragons" (as they say in *Game of Thrones*). HBO CEO Richard Plepler announced "It is time to remove all barriers to those who want HBO" by launching a stand-alone over-the-top service in 2015. Thus HBO became the first major cable programmer to market to consumers who do not pay for a traditional cable subscription. As a result, HBO will be available à la carte to the 70 million households with only basic cable or satellite service and to the 10 million with high speed Internet but no pay TV service at all.

"This is the tipping point — and the beginning of real change coming to television," said Jeffrey Cole, director of USC's Center for the Digital Future. "Cable as it exists now will have to change."

In the emerging landscape, the big networks will get bigger as they attract more online viewers, and the big pay-TV bundles will get smaller as cable and satellite firms adapt to changing times.

For viewers this may be a relief. For creators, if you have a show on one of the great platforms, more people will have access to your work and your audience will keep growing. But if you are a small producer, you may depend on being part of a larger bundle to have an audience at all. As the Internet increasingly replaces cable, and giants splash around in the stream, individual artists may struggle to keep their heads above the water. Of course, that's how it's always been.

CONCLUSION

Whether you write for basic cable, premium cable, any of the niches and genres, or whatever mash-up emerges, the keys to any of the kingdoms are the same: the keys are on your keyboard.

INTERACT WITH CHAPTER THREE

- Thinking about "genre," create an idea for a sci-fi/fantasy show that avoids clichés. Plan a series that is not set in a dystopian future and does not rely on young people with superpowers who save the world.
- Take Michael Lombardo's HBO challenge. How would you reinterpret *Girls* for characters that are not all white, middle-class recent college graduates?
- Explore the mix of comedy and drama in Showtime's series *Shameless*, *Nurse Jackie*, and *Weeds*. Then compare them with *Portlandia* on IFC and *Modern Family* on ABC. What defines a comedy series today? What makes a "dramedy"?
- *The Walking Dead* is the top-rated drama in all of television though it airs on AMC, which requires a subscription. Why is it so popular? (Hint: the answer is not zombies.) Create a spec story for this show.

Chapter Four

THE TRAVELERS

I THINK OF MY RECENT GRADUATES as travelers to the future of television unmoored from my class in USC's School of Cinematic Arts, setting out to writing careers, sometimes with no land immediately in sight. Ultimately, they will all find safe harbor, especially now with more opportunities in television than ever. But in that first year out of grad school their challenge is to keep moving, even through what may appear to be a night without stars; I know for sure the stars are there.

In fall 2013, I invited students from my MFA Television Writing Thesis classes of 2012 and 2013 to gather around my dining table and share salad and their experiences. I asked them three questions: What did you expect before you graduated? What actually happened? What do you think is in the future for you personally and for the television industry at large?

Here are their revealing answers:

QUESTION ONE:

In the beginning, what did you imagine you'd be doing as a writer and what got you started in television?

Joe Peracchio: I was working on stage and acting on TV but the circus would go on without me and I wanted to stay with the shows. I had learned by acting in TV that the writers there had all the power.

Still, I went to grad school thinking I'd have this $90,000 adventure and I'd come out with a bunch of scripts and maybe I'd make a movie. I didn't know what TV writing really was at first. In school, in the spec writing classes, I started to realize that's where the jobs were. I have kids. That's probably the most important thing. I went into school not knowing what I wanted to do. I came out knowing there's a huge television industry where I could get a job.

Joe Peracchio

CAITLIN PARRISH: Like Joe, I came from a theater background writing plays in Chicago for about eight years. But for the last three years I hadn't gotten anything produced and I worked as a barista and a tutor and whatever else I could get with a Bachelor of Fine Arts, which was not much. I really wanted to be a writer for a living but in theater the people who are able to do that can be counted on one hand. They usually supplement their income by writing television so I decided it makes sense to go to grad school because I had no idea how to write television, and I didn't know anyone in L.A.

Caitlin Parrish

The narrative possibilities I found in TV were really fascinating, and the form of television became something I fell in love with.

ERICA MOUNTAIN: After getting my B.A. in Marketing (because that's where my parents thought I could get a job), I wanted to let passion decide what I did. I was in love with dance, so prior to coming out here I lived in New York and only wanted to dance. I got a job in the film *Step Up* and realized, wow, this is a whole industry people work in. I didn't think sleeping in my car was going to be the right method of transitioning to Los Angeles; I'd heard those stories and they didn't sound good. So I applied to USC to find a better way.

Erica Mountain

I absolutely thought I was going to do film. I always loved big budget action adventure things. But when I interned at production companies and saw the lay of the land, I realized early on the jobs were in television. Most of the people who were doing these big budget features were either doing them for the last 25 years or they had their day job in TV, and their credits from TV, and that gave them the license to do those big movies. I also realized how much I loved TV, which I didn't know before.

Katherine Lewis: I've always been a couch potato and watched so much television growing up. *Buffy* was a taste of a great television show at that point in my life. I went to NYU for film production. I wanted to be a director, which is what everyone wants to be at NYU. It's an indie filmmaking school — that's what you learn. But I stumbled into this class in writing for television. At that point I realized it could be a viable option.

Katherine Lewis

After NYU I spent a year at terrible jobs. I worked at an aquarium, as a receptionist at a real estate agency. Finally I applied to USC and going into that first TV spec class was awesome. That's when I realized.

Taylor Martin: I had always done a lot of creative writing, but hadn't seen it as a career. Most writers I knew seemed to have terrible lives. So I taught for a few years in a program called Teach for America. Writing little anecdotal things about my students was therapeutic for me, and that's what drove me to apply to USC.

I interned at some film production companies that were making huge, exciting films. But in terms of writers, I, as an intern, was the person reading all the writers, giving them an A, B, or C for whether the company should put them on a really long list where they may, sometime, three years down the road, be interviewed for some-

Taylor Martin

thing the company is going to do. That didn't seem particularly appealing because the point of writing a script is to see it made.

I then interned at *Nashville*, the TV show. Even though there were challenges at times because it was the first season, it was exciting to see someone write a script and watch it on TV a few weeks later. For me, it's a matter of having some control over what you write and having some say about how it's produced and actually getting to see it.

MATT BOSACK: I wrote for video games and new media, so I came in with a different perspective. I had no frame of reference for what the industry was like because the video game industry is so far removed. Even though, now, video games are trying to bring in big writers for their stuff, they're still very removed. The companies are not signatories to the Writers Guild; they don't play by the same rules as Hollywood.

Matt Bosack

I knew I wanted to write for either film or television. Our USC class was at an interesting time. We were there when Netflix was first starting original programming and *House of Cards* blew things wide open.

Going into the Screenwriting MFA program, I thought I'd have to come out with this good sample and get an agent and/or manager, and by having representation I'd get meetings, and so forth. But over the course of the two years I knew the game is going to be different when we get out. I didn't yet know what it would be because that space is still changing.

BRIAN FLORY: When I started writing fiction way back in junior high, I dabbled in a lot of things. I started doing game design professionally right out of high school. You climb the food chain and I got to the point I was a brand manager and a head writer on a project that won a couple of national awards.

But game design is about world building, and what attracted me originally to writing was character and storytelling. When you're doing game design you're writing about all the background stuff and side stuff, but it's not the core story.

Brian Flory

So I went to USC with the idea of specifically doing television. When I started doing my research for a career change, *The Sopranos* had been out for a while and *Mad Men* was beginning. It was the advent of what we're calling the Golden Age of Television. But it was still a point where the industry was hierarchical. You get a p.a. job and then a staff writing job and maybe some day you become a co-E.P., and you go off and sell your own show. I think there's been a shift in the ground since that time. It's a lot easier in some ways to get into development.

JAMES FANT: I was living in San Francisco, writing short stories and book reviews for the paper, literary fiction. Then I took a screenwriting workshop and wrote a first script. I had a desolate experience at a pitch fest that convinced me that was not the way to break in. It was this gigantic room with people trying to sell, kind of a flea market for scripts. I got this sense of doom.

James Fant

TV appealed to me because I love TV and culturally right now it is the dominant art form. It's amazing what's going on. So I applied to USC to avoid the whole pitch fest channel and learn the craft and get started.

ZACH CANNON: I came out of undergraduate with degrees in creative writing and production. I wanted to go into film but I went to Florida State and it seemed so far away from Los Angeles.

What drew me to TV were the diversity writing workshops. I'm Cuban-American. They seemed like a way to be able to get in without an agent or manager, kind of a back door into the industry. I got into the National Hispanic Media Coalition's writing workshops. So I flew out here and they told us we

Zach Cannon

were in the right place, and it was the right place to be because in features, writers were treated like tissues. The executives will take one, use it, throw it away; take one, use it, throw it away. In television, one, you can make a lot of money, and two, the writer has a lot more control. You're more respected. And there just are more jobs. It's altogether a better environment to work in.

Jeremy Masys: I was a lawyer on Wall Street for five years. I thought I'd be doing that forever; I never planned to be a writer. I was not happy but I figured I'd be an unhappy millionaire. But then I got divorced and decided maybe I should think this through. That was during the Wall Street meltdown in 2009. I was working nonstop for causes I believed in less and less.

It was a matter of taking control of my life. I had been writing a horror movie as people do across the universe, with no plan of how that could happen. So I came to school to become a horror movie writer. But I heard one of the professors give a talk about TV, and I thought wow that sounds great.

Jeremy Masys

Then it turned out in my divorce I had to pay so much money I was not able to go to school. But I thought I don't need USC. I'll just learn to be a TV writer on my own. I'll go on Amazon and get a book on TV writing. And I saw Pam's book, *Writing the TV Drama Series*. I was already hugely disappointed I wasn't able to come to USC, so I get the book and look at the back and see you're a professor at USC. Oh my God, I can't get away from this disappointment.

But I came back the next year so it all worked out. In that intervening year I watched a lot of TV and read the book several times and started writing spec scripts.

SECOND QUESTION:

What are you actually doing now? You're at the time when you're just embarking on something new.

JOE PERACCHIO: When I first came out of school I'd been nominated for some awards and I was feeling really good about myself. I figured, okay, this worked. I got some scripts that don't suck and people wanted to read my stuff. So that was all cool.

Then there was this deafening silence for about three or four months. Some people wanted to read stuff but they didn't want to talk about it — yeah, that's fine, send us something else someday or whatever. A couple of good things happened to me. I had been a finalist in the Warner Brothers Television Workshop last year. I was hoping I'd get into one of these fellowships. But there was silence.

In acting I always felt you have to be really good. You have to know people. You have to look like that thing, be just tall enough or handsome enough or in shape enough or whatever. I thought I'll be a writer and then that part will be gone. I just have to be good and know people.

I knew one way into TV is to be a writer's assistant. So, okay, I'll start applying. And I quickly realized I was going out on these interviews because I knew people and I wasn't an ass, so I was getting some interviews. And I would walk in the door and I could just see their reactions that this late-thirties dude was walking in the door and their faces would drop. There is ageism even in writing. I'm not the 22-year-old kid they want as their assistant.

I got into this place of despair when I thought, man, if I don't get one of these fellowships or I don't get an agent who's going to get me a staff writing job, I'm going to perish. But having kids, investing all this time and energy, going from making money to two years in graduate school to no job and unemployment, a whole summer of not working was really crushing me.

And then I got lucky. Through a USC faculty connection, Gersh [agency] called me and put my script through some channels. They liked me, took meetings with me, started sending my script around. And now we're working together. I thought, cool, I'm working with a top TV lit agency. And then I got into the Warner Brothers Television Workshop the second time I applied. The WB Workshop has the highest rate of staffing of any studio program. So things turned around through connections and perseverance.

CAITLIN PARRISH: I had a fortunate series of events transpire. I had a play that did well in Chicago. As a result I got a manager in L.A. Having that much experience in theater is the red-headed stepchild of breaking into any kind of success. My manager worked very hard with a pilot I'd written at USC. She started sending it around to agencies and I signed with an agent who sent me on staffing meetings during the last three months of grad school. So I had a job the day I graduated, which is exceedingly rare and overwhelming.

I started work about ten days after leaving USC on a show called *Emily Owens, M.D.* on the CW. It was a well-intentioned show that didn't last very long. Again I was lucky. The show premiered to abysmal ratings and my agent was smart enough to start sniffing around for other opportunities the second or third week.

I interviewed for *Under the Dome* in secret. I had a "doctor's appointment" one lunchtime, and went. I was offered the job but I was still on *Emily Owens* that hadn't been cancelled yet, so I couldn't take *Under the Dome.* I was in Vancouver producing the 12th episode and got a call "the show's cancelled." After that I got on the phone to my agent and said please tell *Under the Dome* I would very much like to be on their show. Ten days later I started working there.

I'm starting the second season in a couple of weeks as a Story Editor. I did not expect things to happen so quickly. It sometimes comes down to timing and the right people making calls for you. Then suddenly doors open.

ERICA MOUNTAIN: At USC, I immediately started interning. My idea was do everything until you kill yourself. I was like a workhorse that keeps going until it drops dead. So I took as many internships as I could, including one at *Criminal Minds*. While I was there, both of the p.a.'s got other spots. Before they left, one of them introduced me to his agent and I was able to sign with them. Then I took his job as a writer's p.a.

I was up for a spot on *Grimm* and came close to getting it. Now I'm out on meetings. It's frustrating, coming close to things, always having to manage my representation — "Hey did you read that thing you said you were going to read?" It kind of feels like that workhorse situation makes you want to drop dead. I'm still trying to do everything I possibly can, but it's a matter of endurance, just not giving up.

If nothing else happens, I'm going to try to produce something myself. I still have dreams of running my own production company someday.

Katherine Lewis: I got lucky with a job when I came out of school. I had interned on a few Nickelodeon shows and freelance p.a.'d for them, so as soon as I got out there was an opening for a postproduction p.a. and I took it, even though it's grueling hours. Post is interesting and it's a great experience as a writer to see how Post works.

For representation, I'm in a dance with a few managers, trying to get them to read more of my stuff. But I'm just now figuring out who I am as a writer. Taking my time with that and not getting the wrong representation right now is good.

Taylor Martin: I had a positive experience. Quite a few people read things. And then I won the Humanitas Award for the pilot I wrote in Pam's class. It was cool because they changed the award this year so in addition to money I get to write a freelance script for a Fox show. That's exciting to have a writing opportunity on a TV show.

Also I got a writer's p.a. job on *The Blacklist* through a writer who'd been on a show where I interned before. It's good to be on a show because you can see the trajectory: if I keep doing my job well I can move up. But this show is not exactly what I want to write. I'm working on a new pilot so I'll be ready if I'm lucky enough to go up for staffing on the kind of shows I do want to write.

MATT BOSACK: In my last semester during a class, I pitched my Navy Seal TV series to Mace Neufeld, the producer of the Tom Clancy movies, a legend in the industry. Mace was on the panel of industry folks there to critique everyone's pitches, and afterwards he walked up to me and was talking about the project. A week later I get a call to come in and meet with him. So I go pitch to his Director of Development. They loved the script; they were all about it. They were trying to find a showrunner to beef up the project and take it out. But then I got the call: there's too much Navy Seal stuff coming out, and they'll call if there's another opportunity to work with me. That was so close.

Meanwhile, I'm working with a manager on a different pilot. I've been constantly writing. I want somebody else to care that I'm writing. Meanwhile I've been writing and getting paid for it every day in the video games and new media area. With the advent of new media and all those options, there's this pull within the new media industry as well as video games — they're dying for writers. If you've written a pilot or even a spec feature and you're any good, all these other industries want you. It's interesting to see that. If I wanted to, I could say let's forget this film and TV stuff and focus on games and new media.

For new writers it provides more options. At the same time it will be interesting to see how it plays out because game writers aren't protected by the Writers Guild, and writers don't have the same kinds of rights as if they're writing for television.

BRIAN FLORY: I was thankful I had experience as a writer in the game industry. That prepared me for the peaks and valleys of work in this town.

I was fortunate that while I was still in school I staffed on a small cable show. I was hired along with a group for a second season of a telenovella to make it more of an American production. I was lucky it was such a small show without a lot of visibility so it doesn't cause a problem when I want to sell myself because when I bring up the show nobody recognizes the title. It did give me experience in a writers' room and on episodes in terms of structure and approach in storytelling and character. But we got cancelled before the first episode of the season even got shot.

After that, I wrote another pilot that landed me a manager. It was a light procedural with some soapy elements — network oriented. The downside was I discovered how important "branding" is. You tell yourself I can write anything, but telenovellas and light procedurals are not what I came here to do. I love sci-fi, genre, fantasy, horror. It took me about six months to discover the manager had no interest in the realm I wanted. So I gave him a call and said, look, the direction I need to be moving my career is not the direction we're going in. And we parted ways.

Fortunately, I had won the Austin Film Festival one-hour pilot competition with the script I developed in class. That got me several meetings and I signed with new management. This manager is reminding me that a lot more pilots from writers who are low on the food chain are being considered. He said not only are feature writers going to TV, but also the business model of features is going to TV, so more spec pilots are being sold and made. In the genre world, especially, he's pushing me toward development rather than staffing.

James Fant: A couple of weeks after I graduated I was contacted by a few agencies [off the list of scripts sent out by the Division of Screen and Television Writing] and I got an agent. I had been writing prose before, and I had a book agent before so I knew in the literary world the agent does everything. You never have to go meet publishers or anything like that. Whereas for a writer in Hollywood, agents open the door for you but you have to go in and sell yourself. I like that because you have more control.

I had this epiphany: it's very hard to be a writer but it's even harder to be successful as a TV network right now because there's so much competition. So actually it's a great position to be in to have ideas that people want to hear. I've gone to meetings where their hunger for new voices, new ideas is palpable. It's powerful. There's a demand for new content, which I think is great.

I got paired with a production company to do a period piece. I've gone to pitch meetings and had near misses. Zach Cannon and I wrote a feature that just got a producer attached. I feel lucky that happened quickly.

ZACH CANNON: My experience is a testament to how good it is to have a strong personal network. Through the Writing Division, I was invited to apply for an internship with a television producer they couldn't name. Then I heard back on New Year's Eve it was David Milch for the second season of *Luck*. But over our spring break the third horse died and *Luck* got cancelled. I came back after the break and all the writers were gone. Two of us interns were just hanging out wondering what would happen next.

I went home to Miami for a couple of weeks after graduation thinking I'd have to move on to finding a job. I got my lifeguard certification re-done. But things fell in line. The person Milch had as a writer's assistant moved on, so a few weeks later, they offered me the job on his new HBO show. They're waiting to hear about a pickup.

Meanwhile, James and I cowrote a feature and through some of my contacts at the National Hispanic Media Coalition it went out to some producers and one has optioned it. It was good to stay in touch, keep getting coffee and drinks with people from school because that's how everything has ended up happening.

JEREMY MASYS: Before I graduated I had two TV pilots I'd written and was working on a third. I took the first five pages of that to an acting workshop. They decided to put it on, and the Executive Producer of *The Help* came. After the performance, he asked for the script. I said I have five pages — would you like to read those? But by the end of the week we were on the phone and he said he'd like to work with me and pitch it.

I had to wait until I graduated but then I wrote the script in a couple of weeks. I love it. It's my favorite thing by far I've ever written. It's a subversively reverent look at evangelical Christianity. I worked with this Academy Award–nominated producer and his world to shape it. It was great to have that level of input. They took it out.

I got a manager through that who'd heard this tale of the acting workshop. He started sending out my original two scripts to agencies. What I got from the agents was these are pretty good but not good enough to add you to our list of unemployed writers. They did get me to a lot of general meetings at production companies, though. Guys my age, the executives, dug the whole ex-lawyer thing.

Meanwhile the *Help* producer has taken that script to all the major studios. The feedback was positive but it was passed on. It's a strange show: I was trying to do for Christians what *The Sopranos* did for mobsters. Who knows, maybe someday?

QUESTION THREE

What is your own future as you imagine it five years or more from now? How will opportunities in the industry change? How will shows themselves evolve?

MATT BOSACK: One of the questions is whether the physical cable is going to still exist, and more specifically the digital set-top box. It's archaic technology when compared to what's coming out. Even with the premium networks like HBO, I watch HBO now through HBO GO, and that's on my Roku. That's where the video game industry is moving and it's a billion dollar industry. It's going to take with it these different service providers that want to get visibility.

As a writer, as Brian mentioned, to break through and get into one of those big networks, ABC, CBS, NBC, you have to rise through the chains. But I go on the road and there's Crackle, Movie Four, and all these little stations that have content. As a writer it's interesting to see where your managers are sending you now. What kind of content are you going to be pitching? Will it be a little more adventurous? Will these new channels go after niche content as opposed to mainstream? I don't know if the days are over where a million viewers are around for scripted content.

Joe Peracchio: Agents and managers are going to go where the money is. They're not interested in this Crackle stuff. Not my agents — we're going to the networks, we're going to the production companies. One of the production companies is interested in developing a series out of a feature I wrote. But they're only going to the places where there's cash.

The real question for the tiny new channels is how do they monetize any of this? It's nice that we can all make our series of ten-minute pieces of content, but if there's no money there, it's not driving anybody to those outlets.

Erica Mountain: I just heard a panel with Kevin Feige from Marvel and someone in the audience asked what are you guys doing with the new Netflix deal for *Agents of S.H.I.E.L.D.*? Is it making it harder for new voices to get on television? He danced all around that but he ended up saying it's compressing everything. You can think that once it's possible, everyone else can do it. Once someone's web series sells as a television series, the public imagines it's possible for everyone else. Once a big company can get five shows across different platforms it's possible for every other *big* company too. But that doesn't apply to individual writers.

It seems more like going backward to the big corporations: they say, I'm going to make a deal with ABC for example, so all of my productions are going to be on ABC-owned properties, and do these epic projects that no little company can do. No writer and no small channel owner can afford to do that. That's a new idea in the mix — the power of corporate entities.

Zach Cannon: I had a meeting at ABC a little while ago with someone who said that they're looking at TBS that's putting all their content online and basically making an online channel. ABC hasn't jumped into that yet but their sister company is Apple and a lot of their sister networks like Disney XD and ESPN are available straight through Apple TV. My thought to him was that where the content winds up doesn't matter that much because stories are still stories and you can still tell a story no matter where it is. He said that's true but the problem is you're going to have to tell them for a lot less if there's less money coming in because viewership is down.

BRIAN FLORY: We can observe an increased vertical integration everywhere. New media isn't going to change that because it's just these vertically organized companies adding more rungs onto their own ladders, rather than diversifying.

As writers we should keep our eyes on deals like what Marvel is doing for the kinds of projects we're looking at selling. At Marvel there will be four different ongoing series that will all feed into a single miniseries, like the way they did with the various Avengers movies feeding into *The Avengers*. At the same time, we can't do that. We still have to do the small things.

CAITLIN PARRISH: I want to switch and talk about content instead of platform. I've started a conversation with a couple of studios about me developing a show within the next five years and being the showrunner. That's my dream job. After the first season of *The Dome* I was pitched a couple of shows to develop this coming season. I'm not going to for a variety of reasons, one of which is I don't feel experienced enough. I'm fortunate to be working on another season of *Under the Dome.*

A second reason is if you're young and a woman you are only handed shows that are romances, or given CW quality shows. You are told obviously you must be a specialist in romantic comedy. I am a dark, bitter "mf" who wants only to wreak havoc and write upsetting sexual dynamics. I was reading again and again these summaries of shows that are futuristic sci-fi romance sagas, and I had to keep saying over and over I am the exact opposite person you want for this job.

What I'm interested in seeing in the next few years — We've had this golden age of male antiheroes in the last decade like Tony Soprano, Don Draper, and Walter White and other marvelous programs. Now the female antihero has started to tiptoe in. One of the fears, particularly when you're writing for network television, is your female protagonist has to be likable.

If your leading woman is not likable, as far as networks are concerned, she should not exist, at least not in the limelight.

Now *Homeland* and *Orange Is the New Black* and *Nurse Jackie*, all of which are cable or Netflix shows, have these wonderful, complicated, occasionally brutally unlikable women on center stage. The next question is how we get a show that doesn't need a white woman at the center who can be unlikable. I'm very encouraged to see a show like *Scandal*, even though Olivia Pope wears the white hat more often than not, but she doesn't always do the right thing and has made some hideous choices. That's very exciting. *Orange Is the New Black* is the best example of a complete swath of the female experience over class and race and sexuality, letting different women take center stage in their turn.

What I'm looking forward to, and what I hope is the case, is regardless of platform that examination of women as more complete people who can be flawed and be the center of the story, not just the romantic lead or pretty, continues to evolve.

Joe Peracchio: I was at Gersh yesterday working on a pitch and talking about exactly what you're describing: a female antihero who is not simplistic. The agency said there are so many outlets and so much desire for ideas and shows that networks and studios are starting to look way outside the box. For instance, our female antihero is not white and lives in Tijuana.

We were also commenting on international stuff. That's exactly what people deep in the industry are talking about: international, female, antihero, nonwhite. They are saying to make your show relatable to Poughkeepsie it has to center on stuff all mothers can feel, then they'll start to look at illegal immigration differently. They're all mothers who would do anything for their children. People are getting more interested in stories outside the box.

Caitlin Parrish: It won't happen until a show is an unequivocal hit, which is why *Scandal* is the best thing. Cable television is getting there.

Network television is going much more slowly. I can think of Alicia Florrick on *The Good Wife*, who, after four seasons has become a morally complicated character. But that has never been a big hit even though it's gotten all the critical attention a show on CBS could. It's going to have to take another *Scandal* and then a third *Scandal* before it becomes commonplace.

BRIAN FLORY: I have a depressing take on this. I tend to write female leads, and it made me uncomfortable in some meetings lately: "Boy am I glad we have a white guy to tell us about this." That's been the subtext of conversations. One of the pilots I'm working on now is in the New Orleans supernatural underground and my female lead is Haitian and French Creole. The pitch is steeped in that and I'm getting the subtext: "We're a lot more comfortable having this translated for us through you." That's uncomfortable for me because I never set out to speak for anybody else that way. So even if you're telling these diverse stories it doesn't mean the business side will follow.

ERICA MOUNTAIN: As an African-American female I listen to characters like Angela Bassett's on *American Horror Story*, and I think, who is writing for her because she doesn't sound like anyone I know from New Orleans.

I didn't have the same experience as Brian. With my agent, I heard "I hope she's black because we need more." He's Indian and all excited about diversity. He thought, "I can make money from you."

ZACH CANNON: Some of the content has existed but only in niche markets. MTV had its Latino channel, for example. But something might proliferate back on the network, like Hulu having *East Los High* that is created by Latino writers and producers — the whole staff is Latino, and it's shot in East L.A. Think about the template of that — it's not "Hulu Latino" that started the show, it's Hulu Plus. That's an avenue that everybody can come to.

CAITLIN PARRISH: Things are getting better. If you look at the landscape of showrunners five years ago, it's markedly white male. You had Jenji Kohan on *Weeds* and Shonda Rimes on *Grey's Anatomy*. Today you could rattle off Michelle Ashford on *Masters of Sex*, Meredith Stiehm on *The Bridge*, Jenji Kohan on *Orange Is the New Black*, and Shonda Rimes on eight shows. I just found out yesterday that a female writer on *Under the Dome* sold an alien genre show to ABC, so that's another woman showrunner, in genre no less. Five years from now female showrunners are going to be around 20% of the population while we're now 10%. It's going to keep getting more diverse because that's the nature of progress.

INTERACT WITH CHAPTER FOUR

- Some of the alumni said they'd drawn scripts from their life experiences, for example working in Teach for America, or a family's Cuban history. What sources of storytelling can you find in your own life? How would you shape those for television?
- Two alumni mentioned writing stage plays and producing theater. Choose a play you admire and plan how you would adapt it for television.
- Research the postgraduate television writing fellowships. These include development programs at ABC/Disney, CBS, NBC, Warner Brothers, HBO, Humanitas "New Voices," and the Sundance Screenwriting Labs. All contests are highly competitive and require a pilot script as well as a spec script for a series currently in production. These are all excellent opportunities to begin careers.

Amazon
Hulu
Yahoo
Dish
Netflix
My Sexuality
Look At Me
My Morality
My Channel
THE

THE NEW WORLD

AS WE ARRIVE AT THE NEW WORLD of television, even from afar we can see massive structures under construction, each one unique, as if still experimenting with what kinds of architecture will work in the new space. Some of this land is wilderness. But the same fiefdoms that dominated the Old World have footholds here, and how long it will remain open and wild is unknown. In fact, among the industry leaders, producers, and writers I asked, not one person was willing to project anything confidently more than five years into the future.

I divide the New World into four categories, giving each a chapter: Chapter Five — Empires of the New World (Netflix, Hulu, DirecTV, Yahoo, Amazon); Chapter Six — Skyscrapers (Machinima, AwesomenessTV); Chapter Seven — The Boardwalk (YouTube, web series); Chapter Eight — The Far Frontier (interactive and transmedia).

Welcome to the New World.

Chapter Five

EMPIRES OF THE NEW WORLD

AT THE MANY COMPANIES I VISITED, executives generously shared their experiences as they figure out the future along with the rest of us.

My favorite was Netflix, where Ted Sarandos, Chief Content Officer, came out to greet me himself. We sat in his comfortable office and chatted honestly for close to an hour. He seemed as interested in my opinions as I was in his, asking, for example, what I thought of the women characters in *House of Cards*. He seemed to be open to ideas, really wanting to think about television. Some of the executives I interviewed elsewhere took potshots at Netflix — mostly questioning how they could make money when they spend so much on their original productions. It's kind of a sideways compliment that everyone is shooting at them, suggesting Netflix is, indeed, the biggest target at the moment.

So I will begin with what's happening at Netflix.

NETFLIX

If your time machine is broken you might think Netflix is the place that mails rented DVDs to your house. You'd better fix that machine. If you set it for 2013, Netflix represents the revolution in television, when quality serialized shows were first produced directly for the Internet, beginning with *House*

of Cards, and just in case anyone thought that was a fluke, *Orange Is the New Black* soon followed. Fast-forward just a year or two and Netflix is a place where all sorts of original television shows are streamed to tens of millions of devices, each series available all at once so it can be downloaded as viewers want. But Netflix by then is one of several purveyors of great shows, along the lines of HBO and AMC as well as online. It's a time when it doesn't matter so much where a show first appeared.

My writer friends and I love Netflix because it provides another place for our best work. But this isn't our first romance. At the dawn of the 21st century we were sweet on HBO for *Oz* and *The Sopranos*; in the first decade of the century we had a big crush on AMC for *Mad Men* and *Breaking Bad*. Now we welcome Netflix in the second decade. In fact, when I met Ted Sarandos (Chief Content Officer) I said, "Thank you for existing." I wasn't trying to thank his mom, of course, but letting him know that the creative community values the opportunities Netflix has opened.

When *House of Cards* was nominated for nine Emmys, including Best Drama Series, the *Los Angeles Times* trumpeted: "The era of Internet television is officially here… The nominations gave instant credibility to Netflix." The *Times* continued, this "augurs a coming tide of original online content — a genre until earlier this year was often derided as synonymous with 'webisodes' and cheap, short videos a la YouTube gag-meisters."

The Hollywood Reporter chimed in, "Netflix has become Hollywood's biggest fascination in part because of its splashy initial shows but mostly because of what it represents: the first deep-pocketed platform for original content to emerge since the cable TV renaissance of the late 1990s. And at least so far, its strategy seems to be working." This includes "fending off new, lower-paying streaming players such as Amazon and Hulu." *THR* concluded that the Emmys are "a valuable symbol of the mainstreaming of Internet television. This puts it on the same playing field with the best of broadcast, cable, and premium television and resets the expectations of the industry and the consumer."

How did Netflix do it? Part of the answer is financial. Netflix invests more than $2 billion a year licensing movies and TV shows and creating original content. When online competition heated up, with YouTube making film rental deals with studios, and Amazon launching its Prime subscription service, Netflix paid $200 million for streaming rights to major movies that put the company on a par with any other TV buyer. That was the precursor to their move into originals, outbidding everyone for *House of Cards* at $100 million per 13-episode season (more about that below).

But money can't buy love. Neither can technology, though tech advances made all this possible. Faster Internet speeds and the ability to stream higher-resolution video led Netflix analysts to release an internal document stating: "Eventually, as linear TV is viewed less the spectrum it now uses on cable and fiber will be reallocated to expanding data transmission. Satellite TV subscribers will be fewer, and mostly be in places where high-speed Internet is not available. The importance of high-speed Internet will increase."

For us as content creators, that means tech resources will increasingly enable us to do whatever we need to do to convey our stories well.

Beyond money and technology, Netflix brought a new programming approach to the party. Sarandos told *The Hollywood Reporter*, "When we launched our series 13 episodes at a time the one thing everybody agreed on in this town was that it was insane. I got a call from every network executive I knew who said: 'Don't be crazy. You've got this huge investment; drag it out. Make 'em come back every week, and you could launch new things off of them.' It just sounded to me like the same kind of managed dissatisfaction that is the entire entertainment business. I believe there's a bigger business in customer satisfaction than managing business satisfaction."

Cindy Holland, VP for Original Programming, explained that releasing all the episodes of a show at once frees them from the traditional structure of episodes designed to get audiences to return the next week. "Part of the conversation early on is thinking about it as a 13-hour movie. We don't need recaps. We don't need cliff-hangers at the end. You can write differently knowing that in all likelihood the next episode is going to be viewed right away."

Sarandos agreed: "Because of our 'watch them all at once' mentality, we were able to allow them to create a dense and complicated world." He told the London-based *Guardian*: "We think we can build a better product by giving people what they want. In the world of weekly serialized TV, you get 50 minutes of joy watching the show you've been waiting for, and then 10,000 minutes of waiting for the next one. The chances are that something else is going to happen. There is too much noise in the world to depend that people are just going to come back every week."

Commenting in ThinkProgress.com, Alyssa Rosenberg responded, "Binge-watching lets viewers be reminded of characters and genre concepts regularly, rather than trying to hold on to them over an entire week until the next installment. I'm happy to hear Sarandos talking about the creatively liberating aspects of his business model, as well as to say things like: 'I want it to be the exact number of episodes you need to tell the story perfectly... Some of the other conventions that I'm happy to dismiss: How long does the episode have to be? And how many episodes does the season have to be?'"

However, Rosenberg cautioned, "I can understand why Netflix would want to liberate itself from the creative constraints that have most deformed broadcast television. But in the process, I hope the company doesn't forget that constraints can prompt writers to rise to the challenge in ways that are creatively rewarding."

Despite doubters, Netflix CEO Reed Hastings is clear about their mandate: "People love TV content, and we watch over a billion hours a day of linear TV. But people don't love the linear TV experience where channels present programs at particular times on nonportable screens with complicated remote controls. ...[Traditional TV networks] have to attract an audience for Sunday at eight p.m. We can be much more flexible. Because we are not allocating scarce prime-time slots like linear TV does, a show that is taking a long time to find its audience is one we can keep nurturing."

HOW *HOUSE OF CARDS* HAPPENED:

Screenwriter Beau Willimon said, "We didn't set out to be the first major show to release online." Speaking with Dina Gachman of *Studio System News*, Willimon explained, "When we first started talking I think we envisioned a show that was made for cable most likely and those were the outlets we were aiming for. At the same time, it came to our attention that Netflix was interested and wanted to meet. We had no idea what to really expect of the meeting, but in that very first meeting, they said, 'We want to get into the originals game; we want *House of Cards* to be our first show.'

"So we said we wanted a first season guarantee from the get-go, and they said, 'We'll not only give you one season, we'll give you two. And we'll give you creative freedom.' When you have that sort of offer, it's one that you can't really refuse. It's one that the competing suitors couldn't match or weren't willing to match because they have their mandates for how they do business, and that's a scary proposition. It's a scary offer for a lot of people, but in our case, it seems to have worked out."

STUDIO SYSTEM NEWS: Everyone who has worked with Netflix so far talks about the creative freedom they've been given. What has that meant in your experience? Are they involved at all, or do you really go off, do whatever you want, and then present the show to them?

BEAU WILLIMON: They have access to the scripts, and we share dailies with them. They come to the table reads. After a table read, I might get some coffee with Cindy Holland or Jonathan Friedland [Chief Communications Officer] and say, 'Hey, what did you think, do you have any thoughts?' There's no corporate dictate. It's a conversation, and they're smart, insightful people. I'm interested to hear what they think, and sometimes I incorporate some of those thoughts, but … I've never received a document with a list of notes on it. Every conversation we have is all in service of the show.

It's not as though we disappear into a little bubble, and six months later, say, 'Here you go, Netflix.' They know what's in the pipeline. Ted Sarandos said in that first meeting, 'We want you to make the show you want to make; we trust you.' We take that responsibility very seriously. When you get to make what you want to make, if something is bad there's no one to blame but yourself. With that kind of encouragement they're getting the very best work out of the artists that they trust. I don't think any network executive could be as rigorous with notes as we are on ourselves.

SSN: Some artists say that having some boundaries actually helps their work. What's your take on that?

BW: It depends. Every show, every creative process, every combination of people is different, and it wouldn't work well in all cases. There are plenty of shows that have a lot of network input that fail. There's no empirical evidence to say that one particular process works any better. I would hope that people would see that giving artists more creative freedom is a savvy business model to get the best work out of them, but you can't guarantee anything. Artists will fail; it's impossible to bat 1,000. The best artists always take the risk of failing because, if you're not taking that risk, you're not experimenting, so you always walk that line.

SSN: Francis Underwood is one of many characters on TV who aren't what most people would consider 'likable.' He's flawed, he's not a straight-arrow hero, yet he's compelling and interesting, and you actually do like him despite some of his actions. A lot of this depends on performance, but how do you approach characters like this in the writing process?

BW: I don't make any judgments. I can't. I have to place myself in their shoes. Francis wouldn't see himself as despicable. He doesn't see anything wrong with his own worldview. I think he would take issue with strict ethics as being something that encourages cowards. Do I personally agree with that? It's irrelevant. My job is to try to create a character that does think those things, and you believe that he operates with that worldview. It is not a concern of mine whether people like the characters on our show. What I am concerned with greatly is whether the character is attractive, and by attractive, I don't necessarily mean sexually, although that never hurts, but really attractive in the sense that you can't take your eyes off of them. Look at a lot of great characters throughout history, and some of our most iconic characters like Richard III, Iago, Lady Macbeth, really even going back to the Greeks. On paper, they are morally corrupt people, they're villains, if you had to classify them.

...People who do not operate within the same moral spectrum that we do in our own lives give us access to part of ourselves that we sometimes wish we could be. That's someone who is not bound by rules, who gets to exhibit primitive behavior that we try to repress. When you dramatize characters like that, it gives the audience an opportunity to explore those aspects to themselves in a safe way.

WHAT'S NEXT FOR NETFLIX?

In 2015 Netflix will stream an historic four-series epic plus a miniseries event based on characters in Marvel comics. The headline in *Deadline Hollywood* was: "Landmark Deal Brings Marvel's Flawed Heroes of Hell's Kitchen to the World's Leading Internet TV Network." For the first time four parallel serialized programs, each 13 episodes, will culminate in Marvel's *The Defenders* that reimagines a dream team of self-sacrificing, heroic characters — Daredevil, Jessica Jones, Iron Fist, and Luke Cage.

According to Alan Fine, President of Marvel Entertainment, "This deal is unparalleled in its scope and size, and reinforces our commitment to deliver Marvel's brand, content, and characters across all platforms of storytelling. Netflix offers an incredible platform for the kind of rich storytelling that is Marvel's specialty. This serialized epic expands the narrative possibilities of on-demand television and gives fans the flexibility to immerse themselves how and when they want in what's sure to be a thrilling and engaging adventure."

And that's not all. Sarandos wants to double their current production in all areas. He has a broad view of television and how Netflix fits the future. Here's what he told me in 2013:

TED SARANDOS

PAMELA DOUGLAS: You are opening avenues for creativity. Other companies are already there — AMC, HBO, FX. It's not like there isn't anybody else doing good stuff, but I ran across a statistic: In prime-time viewing hours, 30% of the viewers are watching Netflix. Shocking. Why?

TED SARANDOS: Choice. We've evolved into a culture where we want whatever we want whenever and wherever we want it. Netflix is consistent with the on-demand expectations. Now you don't ever say I wish I knew anything — you just Google it. So when you want to watch something the idea that you have to wait until Wednesday night at eight o'clock to watch the show you want is becoming ridiculous. We have so much great content to watch and we created a system to help you find it. The way people expect to find anything from Google, they expect to find anything they want to watch from us.

The moment of truth is which remote do you pick up. Once Netflix was on the TV it met the delivery demand required — that it looks beautiful and it's on your big screen. And from then it's how do I find something great to watch.

PD: Being on the big screen is recent. I heard that 30% of YouTube viewing, of all things, is on big screens. It's the Convergence that everyone is talking about.

TS: Your TV doesn't know where the wire came from. The fun thing about the Emmy Awards and all the debate that went into it is you're sitting there and watching a TV show on your television so why should you distinguish what the delivery mechanism is. This is just the first time anybody stepped up.

PD: It's about the product. Netflix was the only way to see *House of Cards*.

TS: Up until *House of Cards*, television was conceived to be consumed once a week with commercial breaks. We could take the commercials out and jam the acts together. But *House of Cards* was written and created to be watched in this form with no artificial cliff-hangers, and we didn't have to worry about trying to get you back next week because we knew you were going to watch the next episode in 20 seconds. Then we didn't have to worry about reminding you what happened last week because we knew you just saw it. So what you got in *House of Cards*, relative to anything else on TV including HBO (which still has that cliff-hanger aspect), is that you have really rich, dense storytelling, more characters than a regular TV show could support, more storylines than a typical TV show could support, and more character development. You know Francis Underwood better than you know a character on almost any other show. 20% of a typical episode even on HBO is reminding people, artificial exposition trying to tell you what happened. That's why we just have more time to do it better. Yes, you probably know more about Tony Soprano after spending eight years about him, but we're just 13 hours in.

PD: I watched all 13 hours in about ten days. I didn't watch it all at once.

TS: Most people don't. When they talk about binge-watching, there's a mythology about that. I hope nobody watches with their eyeballs toothpicked open. It's not fun. It's great to savor and think about. But it's not rigid like it has to be the same thing for everybody. Very few people watched all 13 hours in the first 24 hours. But nobody watched just one either. They watched two or three episodes together. That's why we dropped everything at one time because I didn't want to have to make decisions for people and then some segment of the audience wasn't going to be served. With the whole thing at once it served the marathoners, the weekenders, and some people watched *House of Cards* at the exact same time once a week.

PD: Are you going to do that with all the shows?

TS: It works particularly well for serialized drama. I don't know that it has the same principles for procedurals or sitcoms. Right now I know that for serialized drama having the ability to scratch the itch is important.

I have a personal background that led to my decision to drop that way. One was my old DVD behavior and even VHS tapes. I had a friend at HBO who would send me tapes of *Sopranos* a couple of years before I had HBO at home and I always watched multiple episodes at one sitting. My kids get to watch more than one episode of their shows, that's why they're different viewers.

I personally find it frustrating to get into a show like *Breaking Bad* or

Mad Men that I really love and wait a week and worry if I miss a week and have to manage the DVR. To me there was too much thinking about everything but the show.

When people come up to me apologizing that they haven't watched *House of Cards* yet, I say, "Don't worry, it's going to be there for ten years. Whenever you want, just jump in."

PD: That's one element of all the options in television generally, and that's part of the reason this is such an exciting time. It's "all of the above."

TS: In the early days of pay television they took advantage of what they had over regular television in that they could curse and have nudity, and that was novel. One of the reasons stand-up comedy was so great in the early days on HBO was there was cursing on television.

In *House of Cards* there was very little nudity. The camera turns at the right moment. It was a sophisticated show. Yes, we killed a dog in the beginning but we didn't show it.

PD: The scene with the dog was brilliant because it foreshadowed Underwood's character.

TS: No network would ever kill a dog on television. And in that very moment Francis does two things you don't see on television. He killed the dog and he looked up and talked to the camera.

PD: It's not the first time a show broke the fourth wall, but this was a consistent texture of the show, that and the way you handled text on screen where you could read it.

TS: That was partly from knowing people were going to watch it on an iPhone.

PD: The size of screen is all over the map, from phones to 50 inches for the same show. Is that a challenge for a programmer to serve both kinds of eyeballs? How do you deal with it?

TS: Right now there's user-generated shorts on YouTube — low res, short running time, quality that doesn't matter much. For us we know the standards are much higher. The presentation of the text on screen had to be something that would work in either format. Everything counts, and you sometimes have to make a sacrifice. People who choose to watch on a small screen already know they make that sacrifice. But most Netflix viewing is on a large screen.

PD: Looking at Netflix a couple of years from now, where is it going? What are you excited about?

TS: We're going to have a lot more original programming. Most of our programming is evolving to be exclusive. Meaning the things on Netflix are not on any other services. We picked this space knowing it would be a big business, and with big businesses you have competition. So this is a way to distinguish for the viewer, the reason they would have Netflix over any other. So we will continue to expand our original programming, not just in series form but also in stand-up comedy, documentary, and perhaps even some feature films. Think of us as becoming much more curated, more exclusive, and much more original over the next couple of years.

What I really want to do in the original arena is do things that would be very difficult on TV, not for the sake of being different but to expand the audience of television.

Internet TV will change the rules of TV because the scale of it is different. You can do things for smaller audiences and they work. You scale the show to the right size of the audience. I think we can do really well with a single and a double whereas traditional networks have to have a homerun every time in prime time. For me there's no sense of prime time. There's no preciousness of the time slot, so we can let shows breathe. We can let them find their audience and discover them over time. Maybe the audience will take two or three shots at it.

Some people watched *House of Cards* and literally turned it off when he talked to the camera. We're so data-centric we can look at the moment they stop watching. And then those same people hear about the show the next week and their friends say, just watch for a little while, and they jump back in again. You would never have the opportunity to do that on linear television.

Those are some of the things that would be deemed too difficult. I don't mean too challenging for your sensibilities. I mean they take you a little bit out of your comfort zone, like a show set in a women's prison, or a show with no good guys. Who is doing good for the sake of doing good in *House of Cards*? Everybody has a self-serving agenda. We can get there because the show is not really about politics. It's more Shakespearean than Washingtonian. So it's really about the complexity of good and evil.

PD: What is television now? What does the word mean?

TS: Television is the same as when Edward R. Morrow talked about it. It's flashing pictures in a box. It's going to remain flashing pictures in a box.

PD: How is that different from feature films?

TS: It isn't. Feature films in a theater are different because they're out of homes and shared with strangers. But other than that it is the same except you have to drive to the box. At its core it's all storytelling. What it is physically is flashing pictures in a box, but in its soul it's the same as it's been since cavemen. We love to tell stories. I think we are genetically predisposed to fill in the blanks. We're not good at not knowing things so we create stories so we can understand things better. This is why as a species we're so story-centric. The same thing that made people go west is the same thing that makes people love a good book.

PD: As a writer, I'm so glad you're saying these things. From a writer-creator's point of view, can you walk me through — imagine if somebody had a great pilot or a great idea for a show, could they possibly bring it to Netflix and if so, how?

TS: We have a team. There is an agency system that deals with making sense of a lot of noise. We take a lot of inbound pitches. Here's where we're different:

There was something about interactivity that everybody thought the Internet was all about. So then there was a whole thing about content creation where the user would influence the story. In the early days of Internet entertainment I saw an interview with Steve Martin and he said they're paying me a million dollars to write something where people can change the ending — why pay me a million dollars? That's my story so it's funny that the roots of the Internet were really disruptive to storytelling.

Now Netflix is playing a role in this where we're actually going in the opposite direction, really embracing and nurturing storytelling without interference.

I know that every great storyteller isn't published and every writer doesn't have an agent. We have to be able to peel through projects to find great ones. What emerged in the scramble to lock up great TV creators and writers, everyone had a deal. Everyone had to go through one of the programs like Warner Television. So in those cases a system started to get talent earlier and earlier who were trying to sell their stories earlier and earlier. That led to a lot of half-baked stories. They would invest a little bit to see if some of these stories play out.

So if you have a great idea, you could pitch it around and see if you could get a development deal or something. But if it's your only great idea you might want to hold on to it and hone it yourself. Pour your time into this project. If you come up with a great idea I'd say thanks but I don't know what to do with that because I don't have a development system, or I'm not going to develop your script. But if you could get us a script we love, I'm going to get you a whole season of content, not just a deal where your pilot might get shot and never seen. There are thousands and thousands of projects that die in development. Your chances of getting to series on Netflix are much higher. You just have to invest a little bit of the development time yourself.

PD: Part of the reason that's such a relief is writers write. Here's a pilot. In my USC class MFA students write the pilot, the bible, and a mid-season episode so the entire season is there on paper.

TS: That's great.

PD: Internet companies on the other side of the spectrum have told me they don't want to read anything on a piece of paper. They say if someone makes a video and gets a high YouTube number, then we might be interested. They only want to see videos. Netflix is not there, correct?

TS: Correct. Every great show starts with the writing. You could gloss up something in a video but the flaws or the strengths of a show are in the words, absolutely. *House of Cards* is a very expensive show for a show that's just people talking. We invested in the words and the mouths that deliver them. This is not special effects driven. It's not adventure driven. There are no exotic locations. It's all words, people talking.

PD: Do you think other shows on Netflix will be like that? Would you ever do an action-adventure show?

TS: There's never been a great action-adventure tale that wasn't also great storytelling. Even with *Game of Thrones*, what people talk about are the characters.

PD: It's frustrating for writers that some companies don't seem to get it.

TS: There's a mythology about Silicon Valley versus Hollywood. It's real but it's only tribalism, that's all it is. They don't get it/we don't get it. Netflix has always done a very good job of being in Hollywood. We have a thousand people in Silicon Valley — we are a technology company, and then we have 150 people in L.A. for whom we are only an entertainment company. We are in the entertainment culture. We understand what makes people work creatively and the cultural aspects of the entertainment business. They're different. If you talk to a technology company about creativity they're immediately suspicious. So we have to exist with one foot in each world. While we have more data than any entertainment company, you can't reverse-engineer content. You can't reverse-engineer storytelling.

PD: If you could project the future, what do you think television is going to look like, considering digital space versus cable and network?

TS: Distinctions like broadcast versus cable don't make any sense today so I don't know how they make sense in the future. It's just a business delivery model. I hear all the time they'll never put the Super Bowl on a pay channel. For some reason it's like we have some constitutional right for the Super Bowl to be free. I think that kind of thinking will go by the wayside.

Linear television will be eventized. Everything on linear television will be super-cliff-hanger stuff or competition shows and sports. If you look at the top broadcast shows, they're almost all sports of some kind. Occasionally you get a procedural in there, which is probably an effect of the aging broadcast television audience.

The reason Netflix can offer a billion hours of streaming content per month, while linear television is not really dropping that much, is that we're not substituting for watching the NBA finals. The on-demand-ness of Netflix is going to get deeper, and the event-ness of broadcast television is going to get deeper. The real business of scripted television is going to happen online.

PD: Do you see opportunities increasing for creative people coming along?

TS: Yes. More channels, more ability to aggregate efficiently creates a lot of opportunity. The Internet will have the ability to channelize the audiences so they can still support the production of television because the shows have a long shelf life.

PD: Anything else you'd like to say to future generations of TV creators?

TS: Don't feel limitations because it's a TV show. On one level *House of Cards* is a 13-hour movie, or a 39-hour movie. I want people to write the perfect story in the perfect time. *Arrested Development* is 15 episodes, which is kind of an oddball number. Every episode has a different running time. The less they are connected to a linear grid for creativity, the more the show is like a novel. If every novel had to be the same number of pages, books would be pretty lousy.

So writing a 22-minute sitcom you have a much harder time than you need to. Since there are no act breaks, you don't have to write up to the act break and return from the act break. This is more like a book. When it comes to great storytelling, most people discover it in their own time. People see movies at different times. They're on different pages of books. It's something funny about broadcast television. How long has it been since the majority of the country watched anything together? A long time.

HULU

Early pioneers who settled the American West (or conquered, depending on your viewpoint) built some remarkable adobe missions amidst sage-brush and wildlife. Many of those edifices are crumbling. But a few held up over time, and every once in a while an investor type might try to buy one of the things to make it shinier, or even tear it down and start over on the property. Still, lots of people go there and it keeps working just fine for what it does as a marketplace or tourist destination. That's how I used to think of Hulu's position in the New World. Then I took a closer look at what they're beginning to do.

Founded in 2007 by three traditional networks — Fox, ABC, and NBC — the mandate was simply to collect a little extra corporate revenue by rerunning their regular broadcast shows online, including ads. Ultimately, the plan worked and now Hulu is the second biggest subscription video-on-demand service after Netflix. 85 to 90% of Hulu's programming is licensed from its parent companies.

But that leaves 10 to 15% for something else. That's the space where Hulu evolved.

Not that it was a smooth evolution. Back in 2011, Hulu's former CEO posted a blog in which he outlined the forces shaping the future of the industry: "History has shown that incumbents tend to fight trends that challenge established ways and, in the process, lose focus on what matters most: customers. Hulu is not burdened by that legacy."

Well, it turned out they are. Industry observers thought the blog would be threatening to owners 21st Century Fox Inc., Walt Disney Co./ABC, and Comcast Corp./NBC. Whatever went on behind the scenes, that CEO departed, and talk of unloading the Hulu problem child ensued. Potential buyers lined up.

And then… Hulu took chances on creating some original exclusive shows. They rolled out *The Awesomes*, an adult-targeted animated comedy created by *Saturday Night Live* writers, plus twenty or more other shows. My cheers go to *East Los High*, a scripted drama series about Latino students at an L.A. high school. As I write this, that's the one and only Latino drama series on mainstream media (though, of course Spanish-language media have their own).

Media-technology analyst Richard Greenfield of BTIG Research concluded that as a result of their new approach, "They added subscribers like crazy. Consumers love to stream high-quality content on lots of devices and Hulu is one of their few good options."

With that background, I'll let them speak for themselves. I interviewed Andy Forssell, Former Acting CEO and SVP of Content, after the sales kerfuffle was over, Hulu had survived and hired a new CEO, and Forssell could take a moment for the long view.

ANDY FORSSELL

PAMELA DOUGLAS: Hulu was in the re-transmitting business for a long time, and now you're exploring original content. Why?

ANDY FORSSELL: The companion question is why didn't we do it for several years? In the business plan we inherited from Fox and other companies when we were hired in, there was a line for original content. We struck out that line. I think their original idea was we were going to do some short form content like *Funny or Die*. But a very young organization as we were then, we thought you can only be good at a certain number of things so you don't spread yourself too thin.

We set out to do a few things: First, make a reality of what we envisioned TV would be on the Internet: watch on your time. What does the environment look like? How does it feel? We put a lot of effort into that.

Second, what's the next generation ad experience? We were going to do advertising, so we needed the way to do that on the Internet, do it right, make the ads worth more. How do we place them?

So we scratched the budget on original content and decided we're not going to try. It's really hard to make things that are good. It's really easy to make things that aren't good. We have so much respect for quality television, let's stay away from that because it would be a huge thing we'd be biting into.

What changed, what turned us, were a couple of events: One, betting hundreds of millions of dollars a year on content means people come to you to pitch that original content. Suddenly you're in a couple of meetings that illustrate a contrast. In one case, someone is trying to sell you a series from the 1970s and they want a couple million bucks for it. It could be an interesting series, or maybe not. We tend to treasure hunt that way. You think, we have an opportunity for *Gilligan's Island* or something like that. It's a known brand. And next you have a meeting with some young creator who has an idea for a story that never really would go on traditional TV. They just want to tell their story without worrying about network structure; they have a burning desire to tell this story. And you might choose the *Gilligan's Island* a bunch of times, but after a while you think, we have to start doing something that will make more of a difference. How do you start taking a chance on great storytellers who just aren't getting things made?

That intrigued us, so we went back and looked at our original decision not to get into original content. The reason we made that decision still stands: it's hard to make good things. All forces seem to act towards mediocrity or worse. You have to think carefully about what capabilities you need to build and what team members you have to have. So that was the turning point for us around two and a half years ago, when we said we have to get serious about this because there are plenty of opportunities.

As the marketplace for content gets more competitive it starts to make more sense to take a chance on that person who came in and gave you that great pitch. One way to look at it from a business perspective is you're moving back in a timeline to riskier stages. But as markets become more competitive you have to take those risks. We had to start buying in the script stage versus when something was already airing somewhere.

PD: Everybody is talking about wanting to develop quality material and find new voices for this enhanced audience. So what's special about Hulu? What is it that you're doing in your development process that makes you "you," as opposed to, for example, Netflix?

AF: From the start we didn't have to go get original programming. It was an opportunity that arose that we were in a position to take advantage of. We have a budget for original programming but we're "quali-gated" not "dollar-gated." We'll spend under or over that budget. It depends on what material we find. If we didn't find things we think viewers will love we don't have to make them. We can go buy content in a lot of other places. We can be choosy and have a high bar internally for what we say yes to. We don't need to produce a certain amount of output.

Another aspect of our approach is we have a lot of conversations with studios, whether they're small or big, and we say in a way we might look like an odd partner to you. We can tell you what we want at a 30,000-foot level. To us, it's all about finding unique voices. We don't need something for Thursdays at eight o'clock to partner with this other comedy. We don't go in with specific ideas. We go in with the kind of creative we're looking for who has some unique voice that is somehow different, and they have a story they want to tell and the attitude we're going to find a way to tell this one way or another and get it done. That's what we've been attracted to.

We just greenlit a new series, *Deadbeat*. It involves screenwriters who have been successful in Hollywood, but they had this great concept for a series with this really unique character and voice. We thought we could give them a chance to run a show that traditional Hollywood wouldn't have. We paired them with Lionsgate and an experienced director.

We look for folks who have a really distinct point of view. We're also working with Richard Linklater who has a long career defining what it means to be an indie film producer. He wanted to do something episodic and realized he's not going to fit anywhere traditional. It was great to work with someone like him. But to us the key was the distinctive voice and it can come as easily from the younger team on *Deadbeat* as it does with someone as experienced as Rick.

The *Deadbeat* show is really interesting because it's at the germination stage and we're casting. We're excited about it. But we're just as excited about the second season of *The Awesomes* where the creators are way more experienced, but this is a passion project that was never going to get made somewhere else. They wanted to tell the story they wanted to tell and they needed to find someone like us who would say, yeah, we want you to tell that story. We have a development process with notes but we're confident we're going to get to the same place.

PD: In your development process are you going through the traditional route with agents and pitch meetings and developing a pilot? Or are you reading full pilot scripts? At what stage are you entering and where are you getting the material from?

AF: There's no pattern yet. We've had first-time writers send scripts. We've had agents send scripts through a more traditional process. Agents and talent come in and pitch a concept. I don't think any two shows have been the same yet.

PD: Are you buying pilots or orders for full series?

AF: We've bought whole series so far. I'm sure there may be something where we realize we need a pilot, but we try to stay away from that. We try to get more writing done up front and be sure and then say let's take this to series.

PD: Television is evolving rapidly. Look at what happened with you folks coming on the scene. Where do you see it all going in a few years?

AF: You have this new world of subscription video on demand — us and Netflix and Amazon — growing rapidly and having success. You have the traditional linear world moving more and more to an on-demand world. Our service crosses over and lives between those worlds. Everybody is moving to an on-demand world.

If you look at Hulu, Netflix, and Amazon, none of us can describe the offering in a way that would give a prospective subscriber an idea what video to expect to find on that service. It's really early. We're all doing a lot of experiments right now, and growing rapidly. Many of the experiments are working. Some are not. But we're in an exciting phase where folks like us are trying to develop some science around how do you program the cable network or the broadcast network of the future? In a VOD [video on demand] environment where a lot more data is available than had been available in a linear environment, what does that mean about what shows you should choose, how you should market those shows, and how you're going to nurture them over time? We've all learned a lot. We're in the early stages.

In the high level, that's where we're going. Netflix has started describing themselves as a network, wanting to be like HBO. I'm intrigued by that. Is it a network? Is it a collection of four or five networks based on the different audiences they have that tend to cluster around programs? We're trying to move from art to science in those areas, and that takes a lot of experimentation. I think in the next few years you're going to see a lot more experimentation, a lot of great TV get made, probably some not good TV as well, because that always happens. And I think you're going to see marketing change.

One thing that intrigues us is how do you take a show and get it right in front of the right audience that would like it? How do you get to audiences more efficiently? There's a real opportunity there for creators if you have a very specific vision and a service like ours can look at it and say I see what audience is right for that. I think we can get them in front of that audience much more quickly than could have happened in the Old World, even five years ago. I don't know how that's going to change what gets made but I know it will change it in a big way. We're experimenting with that now in terms of different kinds of shows and projecting audiences ahead of time.

PD: What advice would you give to a writer coming out of film school, wanting to work in television? If a bright, talented, skilled person wanted to come to Hulu, what would you tell them?

AF: Writers have to write. Make time for yourself to write. You might write a lot of not so good stuff to get to the good stuff. Most realistically it's going to be on the side at first. We have some folks here from USC in junior-level jobs where they have a good vantage point to see how everything works and gain maturity, and on the side they're writing like heck. That's my advice: try to find a job where you can meet people and learn how the business works. But then you have to find time to write because that's what's finally going to matter.

DIRECTV

You've seen the round satellite antennas mounted on the sides of houses. Those are probably DirecTV. As a transmission service not unlike Verizon or Time Warner, their 20 million-or-so U.S. subscribers (and around 10 million more in Latin America) who pay a monthly fee have access to hundreds of channels. None of that is news.

But *Rogue*, DirecTV's first original scripted series, changed what we expect from them in the future. Starring Thandie Newton as a morally and emotionally conflicted undercover detective, the hour drama signaled DirecTV was out to make their own premium television. It echoes moves by Netflix and Hulu to offer a unique hook to hold on to subscribers who can get programming anywhere and everywhere else.

I spoke with Chris Long, Senior Vice President for Entertainment and Production, at their headquarters south of the Los Angeles airport. The high-rise office complex looks like a corporation that makes billions of dollars on technology, which they are. Nothing creative or artistic here. Then I noticed a pilot script with the name of a movie-star producer on the desk of an enthusiastic man who dreams of being like studio heads of yore....

CHRIS LONG

Pamela Douglas: Everybody thinks of DirecTV as a delivery system, even now with all the change happening in television with opportunity everywhere you look. So when I heard DirecTV was going to produce original scripted series, I thought, you have to be kidding.

CHRIS LONG: We were acquiring series from other places, such as *Friday Night Lights*. I said to our board, at some point the well is going to dry and we have to delve into this. Anybody can get a box in their home. What differentiates us from FiOS? The signal is probably not a high marker for people. It's about what they can watch.

If you do the research for our customers — 35- to 54-year-old adult males and females, highly educated, own their own homes, disposable incomes — what are they watching? Premium shows, HBO, Showtime, Netflix. In my business I have to show return on investment.

We decided to take some slow pitches and green-light ten episodes, so we're not going to go through the process of piloting and focus groups. I said let's find an idea we're all passionate about and go with it.

PD: Did you actually have writers and production companies come in and present possibilities? And what did they come in with exactly?

CL: Yes. They all came in with either a treatment or a script or a bible, and they all have a general idea how they're going to pitch, and they all do it in a rhythm. Different people have different ways. Some are bombastic, some are subdued, some come across sincere, some come across rehearsed, which puts me off a little bit because it's like reading from a teleprompter. We had around 25 different pitches. Some came through agencies and some through friends in production companies.

The word gets out. Here's a new buyer! Some more money! Here are five ideas I pitched to HBO they didn't buy. I knew the ones that gravitated to HBO or Showtime or Starz we were going to grab.

PD: So from the beginning you were playing in premium, sophisticated material.

CL: Also we're a small group so if a writer is going to get notes it would be from two people instead of 30. It's basically me and three others, and the four of us sit there. Everything's a gut instinct for me. If I really think something's good, I have the wherewithal to know it's going to identify with the audience. I'm in that demographic myself. I ask is the character interesting enough? Does he have enough depth? Is it serialized? What is the first thing that comes to mind when you see this character? Do you have a love/hate with him? Is your wife going to like him and you're not going to like him? These are some of the things that go through my mind.

They pitch the story idea. And I sit there and say, this has it. Then I start asking a million questions. What always happens in a pitch, the devil is in the details. If you don't have a good response for me on questions I have about characters — if I say what was his childhood like, and you don't have a good response to that, I'll see you later. I want you to tell me his favorite color. How does he react to situations he's in? Does he drink vodka tonic or beer? You have to know that about every character because I want to know you're invested in this character.

I'm a big crime guy. I think that world is fascinating if you go into it in a way nobody has seen before. *The Wire* did a great job about street crime. *Sopranos* did an unbelievable job about family crime. But there's a level of organized crime in this country on the docks that is trafficking in drugs, counterfeit goods, and people. It's something we've really never delved into and it's a billion-dollar industry. And nobody has dealt with Oakland crime. That fascinated me. The people pitching me had a point of view that was edgier and they had knowledge of their story to the point that there was no question I could ask that they couldn't answer.

That pitch was all verbal. Then it was me taking that and going to our head of content in charge of ten billion dollars and saying I know you don't want to do this. I know everybody's scared and an unknown property is difficult to get done but I think this is where we should be heading. I can use examples from Netflix to Amazon to Hulu to all these places that are slowly chipping away at our business, so we have to think about how to keep them on this platform. My point was to build up enough investment so when FiOS comes to your door, you say, well the service is great but there's a couple of shows I can't get anywhere else. That's the whole point.

You take the pitch. You have an internal meeting. You get the green light for the ten episodes. And you spend the next three months busting their chops to see how well it can go.

PD: You did not go to pilot. You went to ten episodes, straight to series. Is this one of the 10-90 deals?

CL: No it's a limited series — ten episodes, and then a possible second season of ten because I can't guarantee viewership. But what I can do is show a business model that this type of show does well internationally in Italy, Spain, U.K. So I say to my boss, even if it doesn't do big numbers here, let's do it. It's our first try. Ten episodes. Do a good job. And let's see how it works.

PD: Let's get back to process. Did you see ten scripts up front?

CL: I saw the first two and a bible.

PD: And you sent it to production at that point. And while they were producing those, the staff was writing the next episodes. So this is the traditional model except there was no pilot, but instead of the pilot there were two episodes that were sort of like a pilot.... So if you hated those two episodes would you have cut them off?

CL: No, I would just have learned an expensive lesson. Once I greenlit ten I was in for ten. So it's not exactly the traditional model.

PD: You're not trying the idea of downloading the whole season at once.

CL: No. I would only do that if the story arc allowed itself to do that. You have to want to see the next episode. Binge-viewing is hard for me because I don't know anyone who can spend ten hours watching it at once. I'll do two or three episodes at once. Here's the problem with a one-time binge — after they're done viewing they don't have to pay that month. It's an expensive proposition. So that's why we've only done one so far and now we're on our second series.

We get the great viewers and it turns out we're not losing any week to week. So it's a sustained viewership. You've built a property here and what do you do next? Then you have to struggle with keeping the storyline going, and because it's serialized the story is over after ten episodes. Does the writer have enough in him to take part of that storyline and bring it into a second season? He's got to pitch me that. Then I green-light Season Two.

What happens is that name creators look and say they're doing some cool stuff over there, plus I hear they're great to work with. I'm not somebody from the sales department; I've produced shows myself. I know the reaction to notes. They come in to a meeting and we start talking, and they say, oh, you get it. It's a symbiotic relationship.

PD: A major current movie star came in to pitch you. She'd never done anything in television before. Why did she choose you?

CL: Because in our world the buzz is out that we're very friendly creatively, and we're going to be able to do a show you want to do and there's not going to be 45 filters. We're smart, and we say what we're going to do — I tell you something's going to happen, I'm from Long Island Old School — my word is my bond.

PD: So what happened to the star's project?

CL: She wants to direct and executive produce and we're thinking about it.

PD: A year ago that sentence couldn't have happened.

CL: No.

PD: The whole concept that anyone like that movie star would come to anything like DirecTV to bring an original scripted drama series she would make...

CL: She brought a pilot script. I told her we don't do pilots, but we would green-light ten. Why go through the courtship of a pilot?

PD: Everybody hates that process. You put everything you can into the pilot and, A, it's not representative of the show — great pilot, terrible show or the other way (look at *Seinfeld*, that was a terrible pilot). And, B, it's so frustrating putting all that effort into a pilot knowing you can't ever take that pilot anywhere else. You wasted your money and your time and your heart is broken.

CL: I would rather you put your efforts into ten episodes, knowing where it's going. That's another attractive thing about us. Also we're not advertiser-dependent.

PD: So because of that it's to your advantage to do what your viewers want and what potential new subscribers want. That's very free.

CL: A great playwright who has never done TV came up with a script for a series and a plan for ten episodes. Unbelievable material, thought-provoking. It sounded like a show that could be done on a micro-budget. Now, we have a studio in Culver City where we do our sports shows. Up to recently we only did sports there. Well they started looking around for studios to rent and one of the guys said I think we can do it in our own studio. And they did.

PD: This is interesting because it's a leap to old-time studios.

CL: Vertical.

PD: So you're going to be a studio? Not just a purchaser and developer but also a studio? It seems you have a toe in the water.

CL: My ankle may be in the water by now. We also work with companies that help produce with us. The point is — where is this going? And if it's an evolution is it a cyclical evolution? Are we going back to the old model of the MGMs and Paramounts?

PD: What would you say the brand is now for original programming on DirecTV?

CL: Daring, smart, a curator of great television. We want to be the new David Geffen. What he did for music in the '60s and '70s, when he brought all the great minds together and it was kind of like this artists' colony, I want to be that for television. Those are the kinds of people I want to attract who don't really want to go into a meeting with 25 people who are MBAs who have never been on a set. They really want to be with people where they can say, he really knows what he's talking about. That's our identity. We want you to really feel like you're part of something.

PD: If a new writer had a project and thought of bringing it to DirecTV, what would that person do?

CL: They have to think about the financing. How much is this going to cost? They could bring it to me and I could go find a partner like Freemantle, Endemol, or others, and say, "Read this script." The problem is it depends on what has he done before. They could do these short forms — the ten-minute interstitials — and shoot it. If you have a great script, unfortunately companies are not going to back you with 25 million dollars without them having some sort of pedigree.

If a student can produce ten minutes well, they can get me to a half hour. Then they can get me to ten hours. But nobody's going to take the chance to green-light ten hours on something someone wrote who has no track record. We'd love to work with young talent though. We need to attract people to know we're an entertainment company and not just a technology company.

PD: So where is it all going? Where are we going to be five years or three years from now?

CL: The viewer is going to get much more quality than they are quantity. Early 2000s were heavy "reality" shows. That's over. More and more people are seeing premium television as what's really going to attract people for the long term. It's not that quick fix. It's an unbelievable opportunity for young people to find their niche and start writing and hustle and start with small projects. There are going to be so many choices, so much great television. There's an opportunity to do some great television.

POSTSCRIPT

After this interview, later in 2014, AT&T acquired DirecTV for nearly $49 billion. If the deal is approved, it will potentially increase DirecTV's reach from its 20 million U.S. subscribers to AT&T's 120 million wireless customers.

AT&T Chairman Randall Stephenson said, "This is a unique opportunity that will redefine the video entertainment industry and create a company able to... deliver content to consumers across multiple screens — mobile devices, TVs, laptops, cars, and even airplanes."

The heart of the deal is AT&T's aim to supply content, competing with providers like Netflix and Hulu. That worries studios and producers who wonder if this sort of media consolidation will ultimately drive down compensation paid to content providers. We'll see.

YAHOO

In a book about change, it's no wonder a company finds itself in the midst of so much change that they ask me to remove their interview. That's what happened at Yahoo.

In June 2013, I went to Yahoo's Santa Monica offices, where the reception room is decorated with vinyl couches in their signature purple and white under large screens playing football games, and I interviewed Adam Besserman, Director of West Coast Development. By April 2014, when the manuscript was about to go off to the publisher, he emailed that Yahoo is planning a new programming strategy that he couldn't yet reveal and asked that I not quote what he said about their shows in June.

Okay, interview gone. But I'd like to share some thoughts on Yahoo so you'll have a context whenever they do announce.

Even before this news, Yahoo puzzled me. Here's a giant Internet provider that could make anything it chooses. Yahoo has 700 million users around the world. It's also the number one sports site on the web with the world's biggest sports audience. Yet, in the golden era of quality in digital shows, Yahoo had been choosing to program more like YouTube in its early days — short, funny, inexpensive videos.

Here's a company with a rare woman CEO, Marissa Mayer, yet Yahoo's shows have been overwhelmingly male-oriented. It's as if her leadership is having little influence on the jock culture.

It's curious, explained in part by the company's history. Founded at the dawn of the Internet Age in 1995, Yahoo was a pioneering search engine on what was then called the World Wide Web. "We've come a long way," former VP Erin McPherson told *Emmy Magazine* in 2013. Then in 2014, McPherson herself went a long way to become Chief Content Officer of Maker Studios, a powerful programming brand on YouTube.

Yahoo's move to a current-day identity has been rocky. The company had five or six CEOs in as many years before settling on Mayer. Part of her mission was to create a clear definition of Yahoo. Is it a media company? A tech company? As Mayer began phrasing it, "Yahoo is focused on making our user's daily habits and daily experiences more delightful, entertaining, and inspiring."

Yahoo users tend to be at their desks, on their computers, checking email and reading headlines. The programming notion was to catch their eye with a piece of video and pull them in. But pull them in to what? What sort of creative content works in this context? Is it different from the kinds of shows viewers might expect on Hulu or Netflix? Or is Yahoo going to evolve into "premium" half hours and hours similar to cable stations and other digital services? The issue is interesting because computer-based viewing might develop forms that are unique to the platform. You might think of shows viewed while checking email or sports scores as a genre of television with its own artistic rules.

I don't know if Yahoo is considering that but I recall how insightful Besserman was about the relationship of technology to programming in the future, in general. He commented, "Convergence is step one in whatever is going to happen, whether it's the TV networks, the cable networks, and what we can call the digital platforms or digital networks. TV and cable are already in the living room. A few of the platforms that haven't been in the living room yet are about to enter in a very big way — AOL, Yahoo, and a couple of others. 30% of YouTube viewing takes place on screens that are 30 inches or larger. YouTube has already entered the living room in a big way. As that content enters, and you have TV, cable, and digital all plugging into the same screen, it's just a matter of how are you accessing all this?

"Technology is changing at such an incredibly rapid rate. These set-top boxes didn't even exist three or four years ago. And now it has radicalized the way we consume content and the way deals are structured. As technology is creating all these shifts, we're going to see this convergence where you watch something on a screen but whether it's a Yahoo original program or HBO or AMC or anything else, you're going to be accessing it through an app on your screen.

"What it means for this space is that it will solidify this notion we've heard before that content is king. You're going to chase the shows that you absolutely love. It's as simple as that. Everyone will have access to the broadest range of content that will blow away anything we've seen before. We're going to figure out how to curate it and organize it so it's user-friendly. You'll have a dozen apps on your TV screen that you control either through your phone or your remote. Those are your providers.

"It's not going to be about the 20 hours a cable network might program now. It will be about the three or four hours of key original shows that people want to tune in for. So it's convergence and it's going to be all about curation."

AMAZON

You probably got this book from Amazon. Was it delivered by drone?

Hey, I buy lots of stuff from them, so much that the $99 annual fee to be "Prime" is worth the savings in shipping costs, regardless of whether my Prime status lets me see Amazon's new original television series. My earlier book, *Writing the TV Drama Series*, is required for screenwriting students in the USC School of Cinematic Arts, so the USC bookstore carries it. But buying it there requires trudging through a blizzard of sunshine in 75-degree weather to stand on a checkout line and possibly engage with an embodied human friend (as opposed to a "friend"). Why do that when you can stay in your room, push a button to buy the book at a discount, and have it brought directly to you (by a flying machine or not)?

Thus is the reach of Amazon in many phases of life. It's our final visit in this chapter about Empires of the New World because it casts a shadow over all others, more a city-state led by an emperor named Jeff Bezos. The various dukedoms in Amazonia include the relatively small Amazon Studios housed in the Sherman Oaks Galleria, an actual shopping mall in the Valley area of Los Angeles.

To understand Amazon's scale, consider that Netflix took in almost $4.4 billion in annual revenue from online subscriptions in 2014, all of it from streaming movies and TV shows, whether original or not. For comparison, in a similar period, Amazon sales were around $74.5 billion (with a market capitalization of $150.2 billion) through its broad portfolio ranging from Kindles to kitchenware. For them, Prime Instant Video is probably a means to a larger end. As one top talent agent put it, "Amazon has the potential to be very scary to its competitors because content is a very small part of its business." What's $10 million here and $10 million there when you're trying to overhaul an industry?

One of my geek friends joked that Amazon is "The Borg." If you don't get that, it refers to a fictional machine/human civilization from *Star Trek: Next Generation*. The Borg roam the universe assimilating life forms (mainly humans) that become part of the all-powerful collective machine, replacing individuality with the will of the whole.

On the earthly Amazon, the number of stars a vacuum cleaner amasses might help customers choose which one to buy. Fan ratings aren't new even when it comes to art; on broadcast networks singing contests routinely allow audiences to choose winners by voting. But that's not the same as influencing the *creation* of art; viewers don't decide what notes a singer should hit, only who they like best. In contrast, mass "collaboration" on writing a television series — where the public weighs in on how a story should end or how a character should develop — is one of the issues raised by Amazon's crowd-sourcing initiative for their new shows. Should an aggregate tally mold artistic expression? Is the era of the personal voice old-fashioned? We'll come back to all that later.

The Director of Amazon Studios is Roy Price, formerly an executive at Disney. Amazon Studios programming chief is Joe Lewis, who was an executive at 20th Century Fox. Keep those pedigrees in mind as we explore the Amazon model because things may not be what they seem.

After launching their first pilot orders in 2013, Price was quoted in Deadline.com: "We built Amazon Studios so that customers could help decide which stories would make the very best movies and TV shows. It's exciting to see the process in motion, doing exactly what we set out to do. The success of this first set of pilots has given us the push to try this approach with even more shows — this is just the beginning."

Fortune magazine asked, "Can Amazon do to Hollywood what it has done to the publishing and retailing industries? …Amazon Studios aims to compete with traditional production companies by developing feature-length films and television series — with a distinctly Amazonian twist: scripts and pitches are uploaded online, and may be evaluated and commented on by the public."

Price contended in the article that crowd-sourcing is more efficient than the way other media companies make shows and movies by investing big dollars in proven screenwriters, directors, and actors. "By and large, your $80 million is out the door. You're certainly not going to be able to unmake the movie and go make a different movie that people want to see."

What is he suggesting? Is he considering that a solution could be to avoid spending the money needed to hire the pros because nonprofessionals can do it just as well, for a whole lot less money, if guided by the general public? I wonder. Would you buy a vacuum from a company that had never made one before? Would you trust a dentist to work on your teeth if he hadn't gone to dental school? But in the entertainment business, sometimes people like to believe anyone can do it. And, of course, the public knows best.

So how did that experiment work out?

Well, around 5,000 pilot scripts were uploaded to Amazon Studios through their open submissions site, almost all from nonprofessionals (writers who don't have agents or managers and are not members of the Writers Guild). Amazon posted 25 pilots online, including *Betas* from *Sideways* producer Michael London. Viewers rated them and made development recommendations on the ones to bring to series.

"Amazon had a lot of confidence that they would be able to sell content to their customers the same way they sell products," London told the *Los Angeles Times.* "The same people who rank vacuum cleaners or aquariums are the same people that rank our show. Usually in the TV world you're subject to the test-group vagaries of 30 people in a room in Vegas. This may have felt like a beauty contest, but at least it was a public beauty contest."

So how many of the open-submission contest entries became series? Zero. Price and Lewis did move forward into production with two half-hour comedies, *Alpha House* and *Betas* in 2013. But both came from major talent agencies. *Alpha House*, created by Pulitzer Prize–winner Garry Trudeau (*Doonesbury*), was Amazon's first scripted series, starring John Goodman.

Nevertheless, Lewis told the *Times*, "We're focused on breaking down the walls of Hollywood. Thanks to our open submission policy anybody in the world can get a script to Amazon development."

Clearly, they're dedicated to appearing populist. *Wired* magazine described their strategy as actually "a giant decentralized TV focus group. The company planned to use the viewing data and feedback not just to select but to tweak the projects."

"We may find that the genre, tone, or narrative model of a popular show evolves," said Price.

Television critic Robert Lloyd wrote in the *Times*, "By putting single episodes of more than a dozen shows into circulation at once, and bringing its audience into the process, Amazon gives its TV business an air of abundance and engagement.

"What might this mean for the future of television?" Lloyd asked.

He answered, "The democratic aspect is deceptive. While Amazon wants to know what you think of its pilots, the decisions about which ones to make in the first place took place in executive suites far from your eyes or mouse-clicking fingers.

"It may bring you in at an earlier-than-usual stage in the process, but it's fundamentally the same as a TV network judging what shows to keep making by viewership, demographic analysis and buzz.

"Even the public-rating feature, despite being ballyhooed as an innovation, is fundamentally old-fashioned, an Internet-age variation on the preview cards and focus groups studios have used for nearly a century. It is not the case, as has been reported, that viewers are being asked to 'vote' on the series, as if to pick which will be produced; rather, they are being asked to leave comments and take surveys that will 'help' Amazon give the people what the metrics say the people want."

Lloyd continued in his Critic's Notebook: "The comedies… feel familiar; none are out to redefine television… Amazon's 'open-door' submission policy not withstanding, they are not homemade works of guerilla television, but the refined handiwork of industry pros. In terms of content, what makes the Amazon pilots impressive is not that they create something radically new but that they do 'real TV' so well."

AMAZON AT THE TELEVISION ACADEMY PANEL

Still, Roy Price enthusiastically advances the idea of Amazon Studios as a place for experimentation. That was his message at the Television Academy when Seth Shapiro, Governor of the Interactive Media branch of the Academy, interviewed him on November 7, 2013. You can access Price's entire presentation and the panel that followed at www.Emmys.com under "Panels and Events." It's among many other Academy activities featuring showrunners and industry leaders, and I encourage you to browse the archived videos on the site.

When I went to this panel, I felt the industry was welcoming Amazon Studios into the family as one more purveyor of television. Price told the professionals in the auditorium (and many more watching online) that Amazon wants to have a system that is broadly open to ideas, where they can get as many ideas as possible directly to the actual audience, not a small group of people that are representative of the audience.

"That's why we do pilots," he explained. Amazon made 25 their first year, but he added, "It would be great if we could do more than 25. ...Let's get a lot of these interesting ideas out there. I think pilots allow you to be more experimental. If you're going to order things straight to series, the list of people you're capable of doing that with is very small."

Answering the current trend at venues like Netflix that order full seasons, Price commented, "I think you'd tend to be more conservative [with full-season commitments]. If you have a lot of pilots, you can take chances. You can explore the boundaries of writing something more experimental. So hopefully we can find something new and different."

Shapiro asked how Price compared Internet-based series with more traditional broadcasting. It's a subject affecting all series found online, from Netflix to YouTube, and Price reflected current wisdom when he answered, "In an on-demand world the value of the pretty good show is diminished. There's no linear schedule. There's no feed-in show. So you need people to be reaching out to your show in all cases. It creates a somewhat different dynamic. You have to really pay attention to the number of people who are passionate fans of a show. For instance if we had ten people and nine out of ten people think a show is good-ish; but you have another show where six out of ten are pretty indifferent but two or three are really passionate, in an on-demand environment the second may wind up being more distinctive and more valuable and adding value to the set of TV choices people have."

At the Academy, most of the attendees were more focused on their own prospects than enabling access for the general public, so Shapiro asked, "How do television professionals get to work with you guys? What's the message out to them?"

Price answered that they offer two ways. One is the website, where anyone can just upload. The other is the more traditional. Amazon has a development process interacting with agencies and management companies, similar to any other studio. "Whether you take the upload or the traditional route, it gets to the same desk," he said.

In fact, the series they produced came only through the traditional route. The first two, *Alpha House* and *Betas,* were premiered at the TV Academy panel. Out of the pilots in Amazon's "contest" for popularity, Shapiro asked why they chose these two.

Price opened a window to Amazon's process: "You can look at the genres people respond to. You can look at a lot of data. It's interesting because there are better and worse ways to interpret data. We could sit here and say *Downton Abbey*, popular high-quality show that people love on Amazon. And *Breaking Bad*, ground-breaking, and people are passionate about this show. So let's put them together — aristocratic meth dealers in Surrey. On some level it makes sense.

"But you have to ask a different question: tell me about where that show is coming from. What people consistently respond to is a show where you have a passionate, talented creator who has a vision for a great show who wants to do a show that is new and interesting. A focus on that has a very strong correlation to success. That is the best thing we learned from the data."

That thinking is part of what led to buying *Alphas* from Gary Trudeau, creator of *Doonesbury*. Later in the Academy panel, when producers and actors from the new series came on stage, Shapiro asked Garry Trudeau: "You've had a long history with traditional media. What brought you to Amazon Studios?"

Trudeau responded: "One of my producing partners approached me with the idea. I had several reservations initially. One was that I have not seen great television produced on the web. I didn't see how they were going to be able to kick it up to another level. It turned out that wasn't the plan. The plan was to provide the kind of support you need to make high-end television. I was persuaded they were legitimate in that sense, that their goal was to create 'HBO-quality' high-end television right out of the gate.

"The other problem I had was this weird contest that Amazon arranged. It had the virtue of being democratic. But I was concerned that these shows would be put up and they'd just be troll bait, they'd be these huge targets and the feedback would not be meaningful because it would be so skewed by people with agendas who watch. I guess the sheer number of people who came were overwhelming — I don't know about the numbers — but that was a reservation. But I was talked into it."

AMAZON "STORYTELLER"

Apart from their series, Amazon Studios is developing *Storyteller*, a tech tool that simplifies filmmaking into a few choices (such as categories of character types and locations) available within the program. While at the Academy, Price explained that *Storyteller* will read your script and if it says "INT. CAFÉ – DAY," the program will have four pictures of cafés and ask which one you want. It will put your characters into the scene. Price said, "In an ideal future case for *Storyteller*, you could put your script in and have something you could put in front of other people and get some kind of initial feedback.

"We've learned that if you have a project you're very well advised to make it visual. People don't want to read scripts. Even for TV fans, they're written in a way that's not super-readable to a lay reader. So it helps to make it visual, and if you can get that in front of thousands of people and you start getting people to jump on the bandwagon, and they say I get what you're trying to do here. You might get positive or negative feedback.

"In the ideal world you'd put your script into a magic black box and a movie would pop out and it would have a thousand reviews. You'd say, that's awesome because I haven't spent a dime on this movie. Now I have an opportunity to take the feedback and do a rewrite or whatever."

After listening to Price, I wondered how that approach fits with what artists actually do? Real writers, producers, directors, and actors strive for authenticity in their original work. They ask, what is the *un*predictable interpretation or insight into this human moment of drama or comedy? How will my creation be surprising and unique?

What do you think? Consider what would come of the pilots of *Breaking Bad, The Wire, Orange Is the New Black, Portlandia,* or even Amazon's own *Alpha House* if they were fed through the tool he describes. Would this computer app assist you in being more innovative, or would it tend to cap your imagination?

RESPONSE TO THE EARLY SHOWS

After the launches, press responses focused on the fact that Amazon is doing original television rather than on the shows themselves. It's a case of the talking dog: you don't ask what it said because you're amazed it spoke at all. That's probably unfair to the well-made *Alpha House,* which is as good as any sitcom now on cable. But the press reactions point to problems for Amazon. Unlike the celebrated debut of *House of Cards* on Netflix, the Amazon shows had little advertising. Price and Lewis do hardly any interviews; the Academy presentation was a rare instance. And though both were cordial in their personal emails, the PR office blocked me from interviewing either one. This press embargo seems like the opposite of ways to make friends in the media and get the word out about your products — no billboards, newspaper ads, or website ads, not even on Amazon itself.

Defamer.com posted: "Launching a new service is something that requires press — all of that traffic Amazon gets via retail is doing it no good if banner ads urging me to go holiday shopping outshine the two big shows they're launching within days."

Defamer adds that the streaming interface is hard to use, and "Digital players like Roku carry Amazon Prime, but Apple TV doesn't, which cuts out a huge market share of people who are willing to online stream. Make your shows hard to find, on a web platform that doesn't look nearly as elegant as Hulu Plus, and you're alienating viewers before you even lured them in."

It's tough to be the new kid in town, even if your corporate daddy owns a whole lot of the town. Amazon Studios had to grow up. Now, remember their assertion that they would be the alternative to traditional television? "We're focused on breaking down the walls of Hollywood," was the quote from Roy Price. So when time came to expand from comedies into developing dramatic series in 2014, they sought out wall-breakers, right? Ummm… They hired Morgan Wandell, former ABC Studios head of drama. As SVP at ABC, Wandell was in charge of such series as *Brothers & Sisters*, *Ugly Betty*, and *Criminal Minds*. They're solid shows, to be sure, as solid as others made by a traditional legacy network. Wandell called his appointment an opportunity to "help define the future of the television business." We'll see.

In 2014, Amazon debuted *Transparent* about a father who comes out as a woman. *Los Angeles Times* critic Mary McNamara called it "astonishing," and said it combines the *House of Cards*–like thrill of a star doing breathtaking work with the new-world fearlessness of *Orange Is the New Black*. Amazon Studios is a long way from where they started.

THE OPEN SUBMISSIONS PROCESS

Meanwhile, the open submissions website is still up, inviting hopefuls to break into Hollywood. If you're interested in exploring this, go online and check it out at AmazonStudios.com. Under "Getting Started," the headline is: **About the Amazon Studios Development Process**. That's followed by: **Now Developing Movies and Series**. And below that alongside a graphic of an old-fashioned TV set (with rabbit ears) and a strip of pre-digital film (with sprocket holes) is: "We're looking for great scripts to turn into great entertainment. Will your story be the next big hit?"

Under that is an extensive list of FAQs that do, indeed, answer most questions. No need to go through the whole thing here, but I have a few tips to consider if you jump into this.

Two disclaimers first: I am not a lawyer and I'm not giving you legal advice. If you decide to submit a script this way I recommend having an entertainment attorney evaluate their contract. Everyone has to break in somehow, and if you have no credits or connections this might be a place to start.

Second, this is not a process for professionals. In the FAQ section of their website they state: "The Amazon Studios site is not a signatory to any agreement with a collective bargaining organization, including the Writers Guild of America Minimum Basic Agreement. If you are a WGA member, we encourage you to have your agent contact our Los Angeles–based production company, Amazon Studios, Inc., in order to apply for paid writing assignments."

With that understanding, let's say you go forward. Find the FAQ "If Amazon Studios produces my series, what role will I have in the production?"

Here's what you need to know: you are not going to run your show. You might not even continue to participate after your script is bought. That's not how studios or networks function anywhere throughout the business. Producing multiple episodes (or even just the pilot) is a complex and expensive manufacturing process involving many different crafts. Yes, some writers are also equipped to produce, or have other skills that would keep them involved through the phases of production. No doubt Garry Trudeau had a fancy contract that assured his status as showrunner. You probably won't.

If your desire is to make your own series and maintain creative control, and perhaps write or direct subsequent episodes, make a small web series instead and post it on YouTube. Later in this book, I'll share interviews with web series creators who did just that. But Amazon Studios is more like any cable or broadcast provider, not like YouTube. When your script is sold it's not yours anymore and the studio can do with it whatever they want, as would also be the case elsewhere in the industry.

Further down in the FAQs, an interesting issue arises under "Original Properties Submitted for Public Review." You don't have to participate in the public portion, but if you do and you upload an original script here, the studio has the right to "make it available for community development (for instance by... inviting people to review it, by making test movies based on it, by showing it to test audiences for feedback, by making and distributing comic books based on it for no charge, and by revising it)." Later in this section Amazon Studios also asserts "the right to make and distribute trailers based on it, up to ten minutes in length, forever."

Under the subhead "Revisions," you'll read, "If you revise someone else's script or video, or create content based on an Amazon Studios project you didn't initiate, you assign all rights to the script or video to us forever. You won't be entitled to option payments or other fees."

There's more to this complicated process, but here's what you need to know: If you opt into public review, anyone can take your script or video and do their own version, adding or subtracting characters and story lines, writing additional episodes, rewriting the dialogue, and essentially changing your script any way they like. You wrote *Breaking Bad*? Well, wouldn't it be better if Jesse turned out to be a zombie, or space aliens were the source of meth, or maybe if Walter White sang songs and tap-danced, or how about Walter White the cross-dresser? Why not?

Fan fiction has reveled in these leaps of imagination for decades. And usually these knock-offs (or amplifications, depending on your viewpoint) come from love of the world someone else created, not from any desire to harm. Alternate versions can be a source of fun and sharing among people who don't have professional intentions. And you might pick up ideas from other writers as you would in a classroom.

But what if you do have Hollywood dreams and you'd like to use someone else's dialogue, or a narrative line suggested by one of your "collaborators," or if your story is vastly revised to be better than anything you could write? Or, look at this from the other side: What if you contribute a character and story to someone else's project and your contribution is so good it leads the entire development in a fresh direction? In any of those cases, who is the creator, and who owns what?

Here's how it works for professional writers: it's not unusual for professional screenplays and teleplays to be rewritten. In fact, a script may go through several drafts and polishes on its way to production; in television the changes might be part of adjusting to the series flow (making sure episodes build on each other) or results of discussions in the writers' room where a series evolves within a collaborative framework lead by the head writer (who is usually the showrunner). When more than one writer is involved, credits are determined by the Writers Guild.

The credit arbitration process is taken seriously and is a long-established method to arrive at as much fairness as possible. Even among seasoned professionals it isn't easy. I know, because I've arbitrated many credits for the Guild over a period of years. Each arbiter on a particular arbitration receives a package that contains all drafts by "Writer A," the rewrite by "Writer B" including as many drafts as B turned in, and perhaps polish drafts by "Writer C." The designations A, B, and C are done so all writers are anonymous to the arbiters; usually "A" is the first writer.

Each contender includes a letter to the arbiters, pleading his or her case. And I do mean pleading. "A" might say this is her heartfelt life story she has been working on for a decade so she absolutely deserves sole credit. "B" might argue she feels for A's life story but A doesn't know how to write. She, B, completely rearranged the structure, compressed characters, and turned the script into great drama. "C," who has the weakest position on the underlying story, is nevertheless trying to get shared credit on the script by pointing out his dialogue polish is no mere polish but that he rewrote every word every character says and in doing so, reimagined the characters. On top of that, C added so many jokes the script turned from a drama to a dramedy, and doesn't a whole genre shift count?

We credit arbiters have an array of options. For example, we can split Story and Screenplay credits; we can allow two writers to share any of the credits; we can decide on the order of names in the credits; and we can deny credits to anyone who did not contribute certain specific elements, all of which are clearly spelled out by the Guild's credit guidelines. It's a difficult endeavor that occurs all the time and is essential to the functioning of the industry.

None of that is part of the Open Submissions crowd-sourcing at Amazon. Instead "A" automatically receives full credit no matter who contributed to the script. And if you feel ripped off or if your posted work is stolen, you're advised to email the studio. I don't know how many pilots they are receiving this way, but imagine if the 5,000 in their first wave came through this process and those received multiple sets of changes back and forth from each other, the number of permutations becomes mind-boggling. I don't know how they're managing that logistically. Maybe it's pure free-form and the studio stays out of the public sharing in the same sense that Facebook provides a platform and stays out of conversations among friends.

Again, I'm not recommending any course of action to you, just providing a heads-up if you give this a try. For some of you, thinking of this as a multiplayer game might make it worth joining.

THE WGA POSITION

I knew Amazon had negotiated with the Writers Guild early on and it had worked out well. I'm proud to say my guild had fashioned a plan to protect writers working in "new media" back in 2007, even before there was much scripted work in the digital space. High-five to Amazon Studios too for coming to the table early in their own development and arriving at a deal that includes everything any other studio or network would offer.

WGA executive Charles Slocum was a key part of the negotiations, so I asked him how it went.

CHARLES SLOCUM

CHARLES SLOCUM: Amazon started with a different premise in one respect because they had a crowd-sourcing concept. We did talk with them and got them to consider the interests of professional writers in not having other people rewrite their work. Part of the online component is that there's a way the crowd can rewrite a work. So that's obviously not the way it occurs in the business. Amazon quickly understood that and made it an option that the professional writer had to choose to have people rewrite.

Amazon comes at this business from the mainstream Internet culture that is oriented to user-generated content like on YouTube. Crowd-sourcing was a cultural aspect they brought with them. Those had to be worked out in terms of fitting within the entertainment industry.

PAMELA DOUGLAS: Are we doing all right getting our people represented in the New World?

CS: Yes! The Netflix and Amazon deals are mainstream TV deals — health, credits, pension, everything. There are areas where different residual formulas apply, and we'll adapt to those as new markets emerge.

PD: What did the Guild do about crowd-sourcing?

CS: We did it. It's optional.

PD: What professional writer would ever take that option?

CS: Exactly.

UNDER CONSTRUCTION

Tall construction cranes pierce the skies above cities all over the real world. In the New World of television they are also rising; evidence of virtual skyscrapers being formed. By the time you read this you may see them and say, yeah, you were expecting that one all along. But I expect a few will be a surprise.

Currently, you can buy streaming devices including set-top boxes that change the viewer's relationship to television. Since this book is "Your Guide to Creating TV in the New World," and not "Your Guide to *Watching* TV in the New World," I haven't focused on consumer electronics. But when all channels from all networks and systems have equal footing on your screen, the origin of a show — whether broadcast, cable, or Internet — becomes invisible. That, in turn, may impact what you value on screen: the brand carries less weight than the quality of the show itself, and that reminds us of the ultimate importance of content.

As of late 2014, four set-top streaming devices are competing: Roku, Chromecast/Android TV (from Google), Apple TV, and the Amazon Fire TV box. You can get any of them for under $100. All four support the same main channels (with a few exceptions), so the one you choose to buy relies partly on aesthetics and how well the devices work with whatever else you own — your phone or computer or game box.

Google tried its hand at the living-room-computer thing before with Google TV and Chromecast. Now it's aiming to position Android TV as the set-top box of tomorrow. As expected, Android TV would serve up content from streaming services like Netflix and YouTube. As a sweetener, according to the Android TV site, "Google Cast comes built-in so you can cast movies and shows from your phone or tablet to your TV. Your streaming content also syncs with your tablet in case you want to finish your show in bed later." In addition, Android TV would let you use your personal photos as a screensaver on your TV. And you could queue up videos from any connection.

Whether that makes people switch to Android TV remains to be seen. We do know what attracts customers to Roku, though. Roku — a streaming player that is actually a series of set-top boxes — has more channels than anyone. It supports Apple, and both free and paid channels including Netflix, Hulu Plus, Amazon Instant Video, HBO Go, and others. It even runs games. And it keeps expanding.

Roku introduced the first streaming video player in 2008, in partnership with Netflix. In the first two years a million units were sold in the U.S. and soon over 1000 channels were available in the Roku Channel Store. By 2011 they counted 15 million channel downloads. By the time you read this the store will have gone nova with too many channels to count.

How do all the hardware and software sellers get your attention? Original programming. Everyone's jumping in, including makers of game boxes. In 2014, Sony PlayStation announced its first original TV series developed for its console, based on the comic book series *Powers*. That mirrored efforts by Microsoft's Xbox to roll out "Xbox Originals," a plan to create a dozen TV shows (though they later backed off the full slate). Both game-makers say they'll keep rolling the dice in the originals game.

Meanwhile, MSOs (multiple system operators) like AT&T and Comcast are all investigating original content. Of course, Comcast acquired NBC-Universal years ago, so their involvement in broadcasting is established. We'll see how far they expand original programming into the online space. Rumors abound about Verizon moving into creating originals. Are one of those construction cranes building a structure for FiOS to make their own scripted original shows?

The good news is that these Internet television buyers are completely new. That's significant for creators because it's an additional market that will need more product. How much fresh opportunity they will open may not be clear for a while. But in the New World of television's "empires," these colossi are sure to add to an already impressive skyline.

INTERACT WITH CHAPTER FIVE

- Watch *House of Cards* (Netflix) and *The West Wing* (NBC 1999–2006). How does each show reflect the attitudes of its times towards politics? How does each show reflect its platform?
- Then watch *Alpha House* (Amazon), and *Veep* (HBO). Still thinking about *House of Cards*, how do the comedy treatments of politics change the characterizations? Subjects? Viewer expectations? Now, take any episode of one of the comedies and try it as an episode of *House of Cards*. Do the reverse also — what if "Francis Underwood" visited *Veep* or *Alpha House*?
- What makes a show worth binging? If you binged any Netflix shows, did you also binge *Breaking Bad* (AMC) or *The Wire* (HBO)? Did it feel different that those shows already ran before they were available to binge? How might it affect your creative planning to know a series can be available as an uninterrupted 13- or 26-hour narrative?

CHAPTER SIX

BIG BRAND SKYSCRAPERS

JUST AS OUR "REAL" WORLD has brand-name chain stores like Staples for office supplies and Toys"R"Us for kids' stuff, the New World of Television has big specialty outlets. Their mission is the opposite of the "Empires" (and traditional TV). Instead of offering "something for everyone," the brands offer "everything for someone."

That is, a targeted audience can gather at this digital meeting place and discover multiple channels made specifically by and for them. These channels function on a different model from traditional television (though many regular stations also offer niche shows) because these online brands are independent, self-contained enterprises with extraordinary followings that interact with them.

I've chosen two of the new "brands" to visit in this chapter because they suggest the range emerging online. First up is Machinima, for video gamers. Second is AwesomenessTV, for tweens. Both are located via YouTube. Yes, I know, amateur cat videos, but set aside your prejudice, and in Chapter Seven, I'll have more to say about the evolution of Google/YouTube. For now, to understand these production entities, think of YouTube as indicating only a street address of a manufacturing plant; what goes on inside may surprise you.

MACHINIMA

Enter the large man cave next to Barney's Beanery in trendy West Hollywood and you're in fan-boy headquarters. This is where video gamers grow into makers of television series while not outgrowing their culture. To be honest, I did see a few women there, a group of 20-somethings convening with their laptops on couches in a loft above offices. But Machinima specializes in the kind of visceral action fantasies that attract guys from adolescence on. That's a big audience, with around 300 million unique viewers worldwide for all their properties, and almost 3 billion video views per year.

A mash-up of *machine* and *cinema*, the name emerged from the company's early products that harnessed video-game engines to make animated clips. If you don't think it's fascinating to watch videos of gamers playing and commenting on their games, responding with your own opinions on the games (with videos starring you playing the game), this wouldn't have been for you. But video-making enthusiasts around the world created thousands of independent channels that became Machinima affiliates.

"They've done a great job of taking the value of the Internet, targeting a specific group with a specific kind of content, and monetizing it," said Dan Rayburn, a business analyst at Frost & Sullivan. "Those guys have been killing it."

Now they say they want to make real television shows. Actually, they say they want to make "intellectual property." That's a business term for content, especially creative products that might transcend any one medium. As you can see, their language may be different, but their aims are more in line with the current push towards premium shows like on cable TV, and that is causing upheavals in the administration. Some of the people I interviewed for this chapter in 2013 are now gone.

Jay Sampson, Machinima's marketing EVP, said, "We're moving away from these YouTube 1.0-style shows to do more serialized, episodic, high-quality programs." So they've begun hosting original series with budgets similar to basic cable, for example the live-action web series *Halo 4: Forward Unto Dawn*, and *Blood and Chrome*, a live-action prequel to *Battlestar Galactica*.

Wired magazine trumpeted, "Suddenly Machinima is starting to look less like a multichannel YouTube network and more like an actual TV network. And for a company that's built on the fast-twitch reflexes of young gamers, that means growing up."

So I ventured into the man cave and spoke with Aaron DeBevoise, who was EVP for Programming at the time. Here's what he told me:

AARON DEBEVOISE

AARON DEBEVOISE: In our world that is focused on males 18 to 34 where you can see the passion around our type of brand, we look at writers as the celebrities of entertainment. It's not like when Tom Cruise used to drive box office. It's now David Goyer or JJ Abrams or Damon Lindelof. That's what's really driving the excitement — what's the creator going to do next?

Gaming and gamers are very interested in long-form experiences that are removed from reality. They spend hundreds of hours playing games in new worlds called *Halo* (that has aliens) or *Call of Duty* (that is more rooted in reality) or one called *Bio Shock* (that is more political, so it would be our *House of Cards*).

We looked at the mentality of the gamers and saw that it is not too different from fans in general, core fans of content, and those that love episodic narrative. So we broadened our audience. We now have more than gamers. We're really looking at the future from a content perspective.

We're going to focus on IPs [intellectual properties] as the ultimate brand. That IP can be in lots of different formats but not the way you might think of transmedia — "Oh, look at this mobile piece of content that might help you with the linear narrative or with a game." It's more, I'm going to give you a story about characters in 44 or 50 minutes and then if you want to go deeper, I have this short about the female lead, about the backstory of her experiences and why she's here. And then I have a game. That's if you want to go deeper, but you don't have to. So that idea of IP becomes games, movies, television, short form, long form. It's about the experience with the brand.

PAMELA DOUGLAS: If you look at any television show, even one with no gaming connection, there's always an online presence and often some sort of game, even a show like *Dexter*.

ADB: But if you look at the process of making TV shows and making games they're really different.

PD: It's a difference in culture. The word "writer" traditionally meant something different in games. A writer was someone who wrote code. "Designers" or "engineers" were the words they used for what we would call writers. Now, looking at the new games, there really is drama, there really are characters.

ADB: Right, these worlds are converging. It's no longer about the medium itself. For us, we look at that and say where art meets technology comes innovation.

Technology has been limiting in some cases. AMC is U.S.-centric. It has a limited global reach. I don't mean the content; I'm talking about the network. They might say I have to make content that is appealing to 100 million homes so therefore I make *Mad Men* and *The Walking Dead*. What if a network was making all male-centric content, and another network was making all female-centric content? That wouldn't work in a U.S.-centric world. But when you go global, there's enough so the artist, the creator, doesn't have to think about what market I'm hitting. I can really write what I want and stay narrow and deep. Now I can reach enough audience with what would have been considered niche earlier. The technology has allowed art to transform. Instead of saying that's television and this is gaming, we could start from there's no difference.

PD: There's this term "The Great Convergence" you hear all the time. It usually means Internet and television. Are you saying it also means games?

ADB: People talk about everything coming on one device. That's no longer the issue. It's the convergence of the audience, the social convergence. Our view of the world is that it's more of an attitude.

The opportunity that began with YouTube allowed for more incubation of content. We can do something that's four minutes long or seven or 11, and if that gets huge numbers, then go from 11 to 90 minutes and from 90 minutes to 13 hours and into a game. That's a way of allowing creators to use the scientific method. It's okay to fail. That's always been a fear of creators specifically. They say I don't want to put something out there that could fail. It's not like you're so precious about one thing and if it goes off the air you're cancelled.

We wanted to take this concept of incubation. We want this to be not such a one-off random process. We had tried it before with a comedy room where we had 12 writers to write 12 comedy shorts and bibles, but it was too early. We didn't know how to drive the views, how much budget and so forth.

Now we're working with Ridley Scott to look for new ways of incubating the next sci-fi franchises. We know our audience loves sci-fi. And if we did 12 shorts that are each 11 minutes, is that 11-minute mark enough to tell enough of a story to give an idea if this could become something bigger?

PD: Are you open to scripts that are written, or are you only on the video side? For example, do you read pilots?

ADB: We do. But in the stage the company is at today, we're director-centric. We want to work with people who can deliver a piece of content and show it to an audience. We don't have the traditional approach of working on a script. I talked to a writer going through a year-long pilot process somewhere else, and I said if you had just written 11 minutes with a bible and got that up, you would have been writing for a purpose.

We will work with writers and pair them with directors. We will work with directors who can't write and pair them with writers. Someone may be a great music video director but story is hard. Can you take the 30 seconds and make it 11 minutes that holds? Clearly as we move more and more towards premium like Netflix, that's how we're going to develop.

The symbol of success on traditional television was going through the whole pilot development process and getting 13 on the air, and saying now I got five seasons so I'm a hit. Six years from now that process won't even exist, and if you don't embrace the in-between, you're going to be stuck.

Those who do embrace the incubation steps will have learned these little tricks:

- Putting credits at the end of your video can hurt your viewership. That's because they're trying to binge and if they can't get past that, they can't move.
- Cold openings are critical for videos. If you have a long opening that doesn't get to the point, 40% of people are going to drop.
- Be hyper-serialized. It's not just the cold opening, it's what they did on *Breaking Bad* where the opening told you what they were going to do at the end. And every episode they tell you what's going to happen at the end of that episode. So you have to watch because you don't know how Walter White is going to get there so it forces the mind to solve problems.

PD: Are you doing much in the hour drama category?

ADB: That's our plan going forward — long-form serialized episodic.

PD: How are you going to do that?

ADB: In the beginning we're going to look for known brands that appeal to our audience or we'll take a new IP through the incubation model. There are so many movies that could be long-form dramas that have big worlds. But we'd really like to incubate our own *Walking Dead* or *Game of Thrones* that we own and control. It's the HBO model.

I don't want to be so proscriptive that we believe we know what's going to be the next hit. Pilots are really powerful for us because if we have 44 minutes we can actually air it. Every single pilot will make it to air.

PD: How is television different from gaming from a creator's point of view?

ADB: We think writers should think about games, movies, television, every form it could eventually become. When you write you have to write for the medium or viewing behavior you're expecting.

If you're writing an hour series every week, to write it like a game would be extremely expensive. The biggest issue usually is what makes a good TV show today like *Mad Men*, *Breaking Bad*, or *In Treatment* — those great shows as a game would be terrible. They're just sitting in a room talking. Games are all about action, movement, things you have to engage with or are engaging you. We talk about it as cannon fodder. There's got to be a lot of stuff to do. Games have to live on. So we say when you write this, do the treatment and bible sketch first. Then ask, if it were a game would it work? It doesn't have to work as a game. But if there's that opportunity it's better to define the world.

Look at *Grand Theft Auto*. It's a whole world like a city. Then I'm going to tell you a story for 13 weeks about a specific person inside that city. But since I've told you about this city that has lots of activity I can easily say now you become this character and you're moving into a world that has lots of other elements to it.

We tell writers to think about creating a persistent world. But think of linear also. Use the game to extend the experience rather than playing what you already saw. You should be additive, complementary, stand-on-its-own all at the same time.

PD: Would you say the gaming paradigm has storytelling similar to linear dramas but with more stories in more layers?

ADB: They don't approach it that way. The world the characters live in is like a canvas. It can exist as a linear piece but it's not written to be a linear piece. It's multiple linear pieces and branches just as L.A. has multiple stories.

PD: Does this change the nature of screenwriting?

ADB: It does because it has to be thought of as an IP first. A way to start would be to say this is a creative idea I have that I want to live with for a long time in many forms — books, comics, game, shows. Now, when you actually write the piece you have to think what is the structure of what you're writing for. It has to fit. Start with a whiteboard and say what is the experience I'm asking someone to participate in. That's what I'll write it for, rather than I'll write it for Fox.

All this opportunity creates a lot of fear because it's unknown. If you work for the studios there's a low percentage you're going to be a show-runner. But there's a structure. You know what you have to do to get there. Here it's really unknown, so it freaks people out. You just have to do it.

We're looking to become the global MTV/HBO of the future. That model engages games, TV, everything, and whoever becomes that will become the most valuable media company in history, and I hope it's us. That's our entrepreneurial vision of the world.

AWESOMENESSTV

A young woman in a flouncy short pink skirt above high-top sneakers stood in the entry to AwesomenessTV. While a young man (also 20ish) aimed a video camera at her, she read "important breaking news" from a piece of paper: who Justin Bieber was dating. Behind them was a black-board where the staff had chalked their own news, mostly someone's initials "hearts" someone else's initials.

Thus was my introduction to a thriving network of web channels acquired by DreamWorks for $33 million in 2013. DreamWorks declared, "This groundbreaking deal recognizes the growing value of digital content creation and consumption." That made AwesomenessTV the first of the YouTube-hatched video networks to get snapped up by a big media player.

AwesomenessTV was the first of the YouTube-hatched channels to get snapped up by a big media player. Their series *Side Effects* was made under the deal.

In a way, the arrangement isn't really new, if you compare the long history of shows on traditional networks going into syndication on cable outlets. What makes this special — besides being digital — is that AwesomenessTV's creator, Brian Robbins, was one of the first to figure out how to build a big brand like this on YouTube. Of course, Robbins is not in the tween demographic, himself, but through a long track record of creating family shows on regular television, he had the experience to succeed.

The Awesomeness shows are always evolving but I picked up a few episode summaries online. All of these are from scripted, live-action series, performed by actors. Here's a sampling:

Best Excuses — The actress plays different girls who show viewers the different excuses for everything.

Kid History — A young narrator tells people about historic events in kid history like the first pillow fight and the first homework excuse.

The Most Interesting Kid in the World — A parody where Zay Zay has interesting talents like teaching his teachers, ghosts believing in him, making bullies pee their pants, and not being found during a game of hide and seek.

You get the drift: aspirational programming that connects with real kids (at least middle-class American kids). Clearly, Robbins has a bead on it. I asked him how it all came about.

BRIAN ROBBINS

BRIAN ROBBINS: It was really always the plan to begin with. I'd been producing and directing films and TV for many years and a few years ago this kid named Fred walked into my office. He was one of the few to get over a half million subscribers on YouTube when I met him. His agents brought him to me because I'd made a lot of successful shows for kids.

I was starting to understand YouTube at the time, about three years ago. At the time my kids were ten and twelve. So I went home that night after the meeting. There are always ten kids hanging out at my house. I asked them, "Do you guys know who Fred is?" They all knew and started making the annoying Fred voice. Something made me ask, "Would you guys want to see a Fred movie?" And one of the kids said, "Tonight?" Like wow.

So I went back to the office and did something I've never done. I said we're going to make the Fred movie. My staff asked if I wanted to take it to Paramount, because I had a deal there at the time. I said we're not doing that. It's going to be a giant waste of time for all of us. I'm just going to do it and put up the money. The one thing is we have to go fast. This was August. We hired a writer, David Goodman, who was the showrunner on *Family Guy* who has kids and also knew Fred. By December we finished shooting the movie.

PAMELA DOUGLAS: You hired somebody who was an experienced writer/showrunner. So you didn't go to the YouTube crowd-sourcing at all. You went to a professional.

BR: Yes, because I wanted to make a movie, not the short-form YouTube content. And I wanted it to be funny. Fred had created a small world, but it was just a blogger talking on screen. We had to build up the whole world and the characters. He talked about his mother, his girlfriend, the bully. David was running *Family Guy* at the time so he had only three hours available in the morning. So from eight to eleven we locked ourselves into my office for five weeks, and broke the story. Then David went off to write the script. The script came in and we shot.

We showed it to the CEO of Nickelodeon. She said this is great, what do you want to do? I said, there's an audience for this kid and I felt in my gut we could really make this work. She urged me not to go theatrical. She said it's a franchise. License it to me for Nickelodeon, and we'll see what we have. The movie came on and it was the number one movie of the year for kids and tweens. Now they're making three movies and a TV series from it.

That's what got me focused on how powerful this platform is. This kid from Omaha, Nebraska, "Fred," built this big audience and I was able to come along with my experience and mold what he did into something bigger. So I said wow, I'm going to do more of this and start seeding content on YouTube. Around that time Robert Kyncl got hired at YouTube as the new head of global content. We met and that's how Awesomeness started.

PD: Looking at the process, and leaving out the digital aspect for a moment, the actual development is more similar to traditional development than not. A writer and producer sat down and created, in effect, a pilot, which in your case was called a movie. From that, a network — Nickelodeon — said sure, let's go to series. The main difference is ownership.

BR: There's one other difference — a tremendous pre-awareness to the property. Fred had built a giant audience of kids who love and admire him. He had half a billion views and a million subscribers to his YouTube channel. That's a big deal.

PD: Going forward, have you duplicated that system?

BR: It's different now because we're creating the "Freds" from scratch.

PD: How do you do that?

BR: By doing what we've done our whole lives as producers but now it's a shorter form. There's a lot of content on Awesomeness. The thing for us here is we're trying to build a brand.

PD: How do you define a brand?

BR: We want to be the tween TV destination on YouTube. I look at YouTube as a cable company. If YouTube was Time Warner Cable, we're the Teen Channel. YouTube is the pipe and we're the channel.

PD: Since YouTube is unlimited, you could make any number of shows. Then the challenge is to get the kids to tune in each of those shows.

BR: It's the same challenge as on any other platform. It's still hit-driven. We have to make content the audience wants to watch. The platform is different so the content you make has to be skewed a little differently but it's still a hit-driven business.

PD: When you say skewed a little different. Why is that?

BR: It's short form for short attention spans. It's a perfect collision because you have a demo that wants to multitask and also has an enormous appetite for content and they have more free time than anybody else, so we have to keep making fresh content, a lot of short fresh content. And we have to give them the things that are important to them.

You have to get in faster. If you don't catch them in the first seconds, they're gone. In a movie you might have the first ten minutes; the audience in a dark theater will give you ten minutes. This audience isn't even ten seconds.

PD: How do you catch them in the first seconds?

BR: You have to talk to them. Whatever that first thing is, it's got to be compelling. The sort of blogger style of YouTube in general is talking directly to you. That's basic YouTube 101, talking to the audience. And it's a two-way conversation. YouTube is the only platform where comments are crazy. The video ends and people are typing comments. That doesn't happen on traditional television.

PD: You don't call yourself television?

BR: We're not traditional television. This is digital. 50% of our views are on mobile. It's a question of the delivery system, that's all. It's all going to be online. In the way cable, 25 years ago, was when there was only ABC, CBS,

NBC and suddenly CNN and MTV and HBO happened — that's what's happening today. And more will come. We've broken out of the game.

PD: For your newer shows that are coming along, are you hiring professional writers, people who learned their craft and maybe went to a film school?

BR: Absolutely. They might not have had a shot running a show yet or had many credits yet. But they wrote scripts.

PD: If somebody out there wanted to bring you a project, what would they bring? In traditional television they would bring a written pilot and a bible or a pitch hoping to get development money for a pilot.

BR: I develop the same way I would traditionally. It starts with an idea and getting the script right, and then it's about casting it. The only difference is it's faster. My process here is no middlemen; there is no studio, no one except us. You and I can get an idea right now and go in the other room and write a 3-page script. We could shoot it tomorrow and put it up the next day. That doesn't happen anywhere else.

PD: What's your longest short-form? And do they get put together so they could become full length?

BR: Seven, eight minutes. We had a documentary of short-form episodes that we put together to be a feature-length documentary this spring. It came out on around 100 screens and made almost a million dollars.

PD: So if you had four or five episodes this length and put them together you'd have an hour show. But do you deal with act structure and cliff-hangers?

BR: We definitely like cliff-hangers. ... Season One of *Runaways*, a scripted mystery show, had seven four-minute episodes that you could compare to Act One of a movie. It arcs all the way through. We write something like that as a movie so it can be repackaged and run on Netflix and sold internationally.

PD: So it really is dramatic structure, just in pieces. Could someone access them all in a row the way people looked at *House of Cards*?

BR: Absolutely.

PD: Where do you think you'll be in the next few years?

BR: We're a young company; we just celebrated our one-year anniversary. Awesomeness will be a brand that will come from this ecosystem like the CW or Nickelodeon. In one year we have over 600,000 subscribers and over 120 million views. Our watch time is not as high as MTV but we're only a year old.

PD: If a student had a good idea for a TV show and wanted to come to Awesomeness, what process would they go through?

BR: It's not any different from anywhere else. They'd have to get a meeting with a head of development here. If they like it enough, they'd bring it to me. The difference is it goes really fast from there. If I hear something I like I say let's do it. I'm in the "Yes" business. Studios are in the "No" business. I want to say yes all day long. We need to be unafraid. We need to just go for it. It's all just let's go.

INTERACT WITH CHAPTER SIX

- If you play video games, choose one that has never been a movie or TV show. How would you create a dramatic series using this world and franchise?
- Choose any TV series that has never had a gaming component. Expand its world to create a game concept. What do you lose from the original? What do you gain?
- In writing for children, watch "The Grove," Episode 14 of Season Four of *The Walking Dead* that deals with the psychology of traumatized children. Create a character and arc within a real-world situation for an original series that generates this level of tension.
- Take any comedy series for grown-ups and adapt it to appeal to kids eight to 14. What did you have to change?

Chapter Seven

THE BOARDWALK

HAVE YOU BEEN TO THE VENICE BEACH boardwalk in Los Angeles? That's where artisans on the fringe of the economy ply their crafts while a man in a turban strums his guitar, roller-skating past the henna tattoos, fortune-tellers, tables of handmade jewelry, racks of hand-knitted scarves, and a drum circle. It's a fluid world, attracting tourists and a copious crowd that interacts exuberantly with the performers and vendors. And you can lunch outdoors in good cafés, enjoying a sensation of freedom.

Sanctuaries like that flourish in many cities, enticing artists and their audiences with the illusion of an unfettered creative spirit. That's one way to think about the allure of YouTube and Internet web series that don't seem to be controlled by a corporate "machine." Later, we'll talk about whether web series makers truly escape the industry — or even really want to. In any case, no one doubts how massive YouTube has become. Barely nine years old, it attracts millions of visitors each week, and it's still growing under the ownership of Google.

A new term "prosumer" is used to describe many (though not all) amateur makers of digital series. It refers to producer/consumers who post videos that sometimes become popular with thousands of fans. But in interviewing professionals who make scripted shows for online viewing, I discovered a very different profile.

The kid shooting a quick gag on his iPhone is not making a scripted web series. Even the lowest budget episodic show requires the sophistication to raise funds (via Kickstarter or elsewhere), and most of all, to assemble and manage a cast and crew, even if the workers are unpaid friends. Sure, the production demands are not on the level of *Game of Thrones*, or even *In Treatment* (that was two talking heads in a single location), but many lone makers of web series work as hard as mainstream producers. And, despite the stereotype, no one I interviewed turned out to be a kid.

On Facebook, actor-producer Wil Wheaton reposted an expression of frustration and determination by one of his friends under the heading "Better to be out in front of the revolution than scrambling to keep up." I'm quoting from it here because it presents the viewpoint of web creators so clearly:

"I remember a time, in the not too distant past, when we'd feel like we had to justify ourselves for making a web series, like it wasn't *real* TV or film. It was like we were creating for online because we couldn't make it in the big leagues, and had to seek out an alternative. In some ways, that was true, because in the traditional way of doing things, we had to appeal to gatekeepers at networks and mid-level development executives who were more afraid of losing their jobs than they were excited to make something new. That makes sense: there's a shitload of money at stake for most productions, and it's only logical that the people in charge of spending that money would be risk-averse. But what's the point of being in a creative industry if you're not willing to take some creative risks?

"That's where the Internet came in, and fundamentally changed everything for creators. We could take risks, we could make content that maybe wouldn't appeal to tens of millions of people, but would appeal to hundreds of thousands. We didn't need to compete with other creators for ratings during a narrow broadcast window, because we understood that our audiences would watch our stuff on *their* terms, when and where and how they wanted to. We understood that the world was changing and people would be watching programming on smartphones and tablets, frequently time shifted for their convenience. We knew that because *we were those people*."

THE OVERVIEW

So I set out to explore the new world of do-it-yourself scripted shows online. I've never been involved with a web series. My career as a writer of television drama has been with studios that made shows for networks and cable where we writers didn't have to go out and raise the budget; we were well paid according to Guild norms, as were the experienced directors and actors. We assumed millions of people would view our shows, and we'd contend for well-known awards. All that is still happening, especially in the Old World, as you read in earlier chapters. But in the digital world, all that seems long ago.

Where do you start with so many channels available? I spoke with Michael Ajakwe who founded "WebFest," the Los Angeles Web Series Festival. Now in its fifth year, it has expanded to similar festivals in other cities. Ajakwe told me he has screened thousands of series to choose the best for his festival. His humor was unintended when he commented, "Half of them are not that bad." Wait — before you chuckle, ask yourself how many movies and regular television shows are pretty awful too. All it takes is a few winners to turn attention to the potential here, and that's his mission.

Ajakwe's credits include the Fox TV show *Martin*, where he was a writer for two years, followed by stints on staffs of other shows, and finally *The Brothers Garcia* on Nickelodeon where he became the Head Writer. So I had to ask, "With all those traditional credits, why go to web series?"

MICHAEL AJAKWE

MICHAEL AJAKWE: It's true — I'm one of the fortunate ones to be able to make a living as a writer. But I do it all. It's all writing and creating — it's expression.

When I was starting, around 2006, I spent a year watching every web series I could find. That led to coming up with my own web series. I learned the shows had to be short,

and they focused on a moment versus having a big arc. They still had to have a beginning, middle, and end. Web stories are just like all the others — even commercials have beginnings, middles, and ends. Dramatic structure still applies. Everything is just shorter. Comedies are five, six minutes long; dramas are seven, eight, nine, minutes long. The only difference between a TV series and web series that are on now is length.

A lot of people in traditional television were poo-pooing web series. But what any writer knows is that it's much more difficult to write short than to write long. You have less time to set things up. You have to get to the point. No fat. The shorter it is, the tighter it is. A lot of traditional television and movie writers dismiss web series as if they're not real writing but I knew better.

Web series have become an amazing tool to show people what you can do. Hollywood is a closed shop, really hard to break into. Before web series, you would write a script or put on a play. A play was the cheapest thing you could do to show yourself as a writer. You put it on and invited the industry and kept it up as long as possible. But even if you had it going for months, the difficulty was getting these people who were busy all day to leave their studios and come. Now with web series you don't have that problem. You can send a postcard with a link to the web series and they can watch it. There's no problem with sending unsolicited scripts like before because the Internet is for everyone and everyone can see it.

PD: Why go from making your own web show to a festival?

MA: I kept seeing all these other shows and I said somebody ought to get us all together as a community under one roof and support each other. I kept waiting for an announcement that someone had formed a group, and no one did. I thought what does it take? I announced the festival in early 2010 and we had hundreds of submissions. The last weekend in March, in a small theater, maybe 1,000 people came through. They were so happy to receive some form of recognition for their work.

PD: Five years later, how many people watch your series and others in your festival?

MA: YouTube allows you to track everybody that's ever looked at what you posted. Among all 12 episodes of my series *Basketball Wives*, on the web completely, around 50,000 people have looked at an episode. Just because it doesn't have millions of viewers doesn't mean it isn't a good show. I see web series as source material that can be monetized in other mediums as is done with fiction and plays.

I took my skill from television and reinvented my web series as a television series. I was able to bunch the web episodes and let potential investors see a sample they could enjoy and get $50,000 here, $20,000 there for a full television series. These were private investors who I knew had the personal resources, and I ultimately raised a million dollars.

PD: So do you think the future of web series is to move off the web onto cable channels or elsewhere?

MA: I tell people we shouldn't look at the web any differently from a newspaper article or a play or a traditional television show. With web series, some people get stuck in one episode and think small. You can't think small. You have to value the content. Everything is on the web now.

That's why we shouldn't look at the web as our only destination. Right now we're calling them web series but I predict in the future we'll be calling them something else like Short TV or Fast Food TV. Web series are just a shorter version of television shows.

PD: What is your vision of your own future two, three, even five years down the line? What do you see yourself doing as a writer-producer?

MA: I see myself celebrating the 100th episode of my TV series *Basketball Wives* that was based on my web series. I also see the festival being the biggest in the world. And I'll have a deal with a studio to adapt some of these short web series into TV shows and films. I'd like to legitimize this medium because the future is now, and to be recognized like plays or music as a legitimate form of entertainment, not just some novelty.

There's a common myth about web series that people making web series are not trained, they're amateurs; they don't have the skills, don't know what they're doing, just pointing the camera. Some are amateurs, but I found most are not. They went to film school and studied film and television and screenwriting, but they could not get a job in the business. They took a day job to hold them over. The day job became a career. They got a house, got married, had kids, so they couldn't quit the job. So they slowly gave up on their dream. Well, here come these web series. The cost of production has dropped; you can teach yourself to edit on your laptop. Filmmaking is not a rich man's game anymore. Those are the people making shows that blow me away. This is the second chance for them to live their dream.

KICKSTARTER

Many writer-producers have ventured to the web looking for aesthetic freedom by escaping from a money-driven culture. But unless they were personally wealthy or had connections to investors, as did Michael Ajakwe, they found themselves even more involved in chasing money. Ironically, the trail to personal expression turned into a hard road to being entrepreneurs that left them little time for being artists. That doesn't mean the business side of creating a television series is without value.

I introduce you to an amazingly aggressive entrepreneur, Matt King, whose career as an actor allowed him to make the pilot for his web series *World of Steam* without needing a financial return for himself. Coming at his subject through analyzing a large, specialized "Steampunk" fan base, every step was thoroughly researched. I asked him to share what he discovered about how to succeed with a Kickstarter campaign.

MATT KING

MATT KING: If you have an idea that's on the outskirts, that's more genre, something that hasn't been developed yet, and you don't have a "Medici" that's willing to invest in you, then where do you go? That's why I decided to go to Kickstarter and create a whole new environment where I could find a million Medicis who would help me out.

PAMELA DOUGLAS: Would you explain your process with Kickstarter?

MK: Kickstarter is a crowd-funding website that allows people to state they have an idea within a single forum — whether it's technology or entertainment or design — and tell people about their idea in the Kickstarter format. People can choose to endorse or not endorse that idea.

You incentivize, much like a public radio fund drive or backers. You say if you endorse me in this moment I will give you a DVD or a piece of swag or the product itself. Now Kickstarter is turning into pre-sales in a way. You're giving them a portion of the production and turning them into the smallest producer possible. You're using people in aggregate to support your production. Kickstarter is the way I want to promote my show.

I realized Kickstarter lives or dies on three things — it's a triangle: it's star-driven, or the newest coolest thing nobody has heard about, or it's something sentimental. So Zac Braff does his movie and it makes a million dollars. The Dell ice cream scoop invents itself and decides to come out, or GoldiBlox engineering for girls says this is what we want to do. Or the sentimental route — my friend has a disease and wants to walk the Appalachian Trail. If you can hit two of those you're guaranteed success on Kickstarter.

Now, how do you do that with a television show that nobody's heard about? In order to create a grassroots movement to put me through Kickstarter I had to have a set of fans going into it. So I decided to channel social media to that purpose. Social media, like an agent or manager, is a way to have your name said in certain circles. We don't know who the people are going to be for our movement. We don't know who controls the right circles. All we can do is get our words out to the greatest number of people as possible, and if we can find the tipping points we can move the ball.

I needed at least 6,000 people on Facebook saying my name over and over again. I decided to go to individuals within social media and use them to drive the bus. Facebook is largely about connectivity over an image. I started driving images of what I wanted to create onto Facebook.

I went around to everybody who could be within this small niche of Steampunk-ism and said look, this is what I'm doing. Then I went to Pinterest and Tumblr and Twitter and Instagram and YouTube, hitting each with individual content tailored for each of those social media. Every day, every hour, depending on the peak times of those social media… Every Thursday, from one to four p.m. if you're not putting out content on Facebook, you're dying. Every Saturday, make sure you're putting out content from two to three.… I made sure I was in front of their eyes when people took their lunch breaks. I made sure our content just drove and drove and drove and drove.

My goal was 6,000 "likes" on Facebook. I was lucky enough that some amazingly talented people within the social media sphere caught on to the idea and we sold it through. By the time we walked into Kickstarter, we had 20,000 "likes" on Facebook. Now, each "like" correlates to a certain number of eyes. Each "like" is a person who has a certain number of friends. Facebook takes each of those into account and keeps track of them. So I would know week-to-week how many people were actively talking about my show. Maybe I was getting out to 800,000 eyes that week, and then I could use those eyes to drive into different formats. At its essence, it was really marketing.

With that in place we went to Kickstarter. I hit two out of three on the triangle. I tried to hit three out of three by saying, here's me. I'm a small, independent filmmaker. I'm just like you, but I'm doing something you're not doing. I want to make something that I love.

So it went from people saying, oh he's niche and cute to people saying, oh wait, look at who is involved — people who won Emmys. I could load this with stars, but I didn't know if that would necessarily push the ball. What I said was I want to load this with stars on the production side, and here are people who make good stuff, and we're going to make good stuff for you.

I did my research. I went to KickTraq. I tracked everything that was possibly like my piece and I did a month of research into why did these things fail and why did these others succeed. Who do you need at what day at what time to make them get more money? I drove it. Every day for 30 days I made sure we had new content on every bit of social media.

People like being saviors. They like to come in at the very last minute to save the project. Once we had Kickstarter in place and we had people excited about our concept, we told Kickstarter, you can help us get over the edge with this, and then you could take us even further. We had asked for $70,000. We ended up with $130,000. All that went into creating this production.

$130,000 is a lot for a web series. But it's not a lot if you're trying to pay a major composer and other people who work for a living. All of them donated their time, working after their 60-hour weeks, and worked for parts, materials, and hard drives. And that still was choking our budget.

We also had to get out a great deal of swag. We had to put in the budget that we had to become exporters. For the first half of this year I was an exporter. I was dealing with manufacturing and making sure all the T-shirts and all the necklaces were done on top of doing all the preproduction for the show.

I still think what I'm doing is traditional television. I'm just doing it all myself. What the Internet has provided me is the tools to do it all myself.

PD: What do you mean when you say it's traditional television?

MK: I'm following the same rules of disseminating things out to people. I'm doing the same rules in marketing and creating content. The only difference is I'm not going to someone who has laid those channels in place, CBS, ABC, NBC, Warner Brothers, or whoever. They have a lot more facility in being able to get things out to people. But what the Internet has let me do is be directly in people's laps. My goal next is how do we take this show, now that we have it, and turn our channel into ABC, NBC, or CBS? That's the next goal.

PD: In your own show, you've done the pilot and how many are you doing?

MK: It's how many we can afford, right now. My budget per show should be in the $300,000 range. My budget per show has been to date around $40,000. That's because of people working for free. We were also gifted $30,000 worth of props for the first episode. It becomes how many favors do I really have.

I can afford two more episodes. I want to do six; I have scripts for ten. Other writers did some of them on the new media contracts offered by the guilds. I'm not paying anyone residuals — there aren't any. I said to them, you're not getting paid anyway to do anything else right now, so why not get a few hundred bucks to do this.

PD: Do you think your show is a precursor to shows like it?

MK: I hope it's a precursor to shows like it. As an Asian-American actor there are two ways to react. You can say why not me? You can resist and say I should get more than that guy. Or you can hope that other guy succeeds because a rising tide raises all boats.

I think this is the Wild West for entertainment, the Wild West for being an artist. I think it's one of the best times to be an artist ever.

ENTER THE EXECUTIVE PRODUCERS

Creators of digital series form a spectrum of experience, a continuum, rather than dividing into sharp categories. But executive producers who have run network shows have been migrating online for a while, and they really are different from the do-it-yourself pioneers. The E.P.'s don't need Kickstarter. They arrive with funding, or are financed through one of the larger YouTube channels. We previewed an aspect of that with Machinima and AwesomenessTV in Chapter Six.

Like those two, Geek & Sundry is a commercial YouTube channel and multimedia production company. Launched in 2012 by actress Felicia Day, it was part of YouTube's $100 million dollar initiative, funded by Google to bring original content onto YouTube, meant to kick-start Google TV. At the time, *Forbes* magazine suggested that "if successful, it could help blaze a trail for the future of network television."

Since then, so many trails have been blazed the whole frontier is on fire. The explosion can be overwhelming, so I'll focus now on one creator: Amy Berg.

AMY BERG

Formerly on *Leverage* (TNT), and *Person of Interest* (CBS), and Co-Executive Producer on *Eureka* (Syfy), Amy Berg was in a position to negotiate a new model of ownership. Her company, Bergopolis, is a co-owner (with Geek & Sundry) of her original series *Caper*. She told me, "I had to hire lawyers to create a contract from scratch because this model does not exist anywhere yet. I'm coming in with a level of experience and the attitude I'm going to make this thing — do you want to be the distributor?"

Caper, which premiered in 2014, combines live action with "motion comics." In itself, that is experimental, using a comic book artist to draw interstitials that are integrated with live action. Expectations for the series are grand. Here's how it came about:

AMY BERG: This is the new frontier now. I'm still a television writer and I will always be a television writer. I don't know how to make web series. I only know how to make television series. So that's what I made.

PAMELA DOUGLAS: How did you first get into doing this digital series?

AB: I'd been friends with Felicia Day [owner of Geek & Sundry] for years since I hired her as an actress for a guest spot on *Eureka*. I'd been a fan of *The Guild*, which was the first web series that existed. So I had huge respect for her as a producer who could get stuff done. Over the course of years whenever we had lunch we said one of these days we should get together and do a web series. I was always working. I just didn't have time.

Earlier this year I shot a pilot for TNT, and that reinvigorated my passion to make things that are my own. It did not get a green light, though we'd

The cast of *Caper*

been under the impression it was going to go. So I had not made a backup plan for staffing. Suddenly I was presented with time in spring 2013.

I had a lunch planned with Felicia and the night before my friend Mike Sizemore, who is also a writer, and I were throwing around ideas. So when we went to that lunch I started talking about my passion for doing something that was mine after spending so many years writing other people's ideas. Felicia said this is good timing because we're in development season for Geek & Sundry on YouTube. We pitched it to her over the lunch and by the end of the lunch we had a show.

PD: How is this different from a conversation you might have had with someone at a cable channel?

AB: In traditional outlets nothing happens that quickly, and it never feels like two creative entities coming together to decide to make things. It always feels like you're coming in to what you know is going to be a long, arduous process. You come up with an idea for something. You go and pitch it. They may not like it. If they like it, it goes to a next step, writing the script. Then there's a whole set of notes. If they like the script, they make the pilot, and then there's a whole other process. They have to decide whether or not they want to air the pilot. It takes a long time and the odds of actually making the thing, at the end of all this, are very slim.

The Internet is a whole new frontier. It's the future. I wanted to get a foothold on the web as a creator and it all came together at the right time. It happened the way it's supposed to happen — people come together, they think it's a great idea, and they do it.

PD: Does Felicia Day finance the shows on her channel?

AB: Yes, it's just like any other kind of network. They have funding through YouTube. They budget their shows, so they give you a set amount of money. My company produces it. So they hand the money over to me to make the thing. So it feels like you're the studio. Not only do you eliminate all the studio notes, but you also eliminate any sort of go-between.

PD: On the other hand, the budgets are much smaller.

AB: They're technically called "micro-budgets." I can't say the actual number.

PD: Would you say less than a million dollars for the season?

AB: Way less than a million dollars. It's around what you would get to produce one day on an episode of a network television show, in the vicinity of low six figures.

PD: How do you manage on that?

AB: You call in every favor you have. That's what I did.

PD: But you can't continue that way.

AB: I can't make a Season Two with the same model I had for Season One. Season One was nine episodes at ten minutes each.

PD: Sometimes those ten-minute episodes are made to be binged so people might actually be watching them in conventional terms — like 30-minute episodes, or an hour. Are people really stopping at each ten minutes?

AB: We air it like a television show, once every week for nine weeks.

Someone could wait until all nine episodes are on and watch them all at once, which is like waiting for something to come out on DVD. But this is very much the television model in every respect except for time and money. We have to do it faster and for less money.

PD: How does the ten-minute module feel for storytelling as opposed to the hour shows you've written before?

AB: They're very different. Telling a beginning, middle, and end in ten minutes is not ideal, but it's doable. It just requires using different muscles. Everything needs to be sped up. You can't dally or do long scenes of people talking to each other. Things need to fly. That's another part of writing for the web that's different. You're writing for an audience with a small attention span.

PD: I keep hearing that. I wonder if it's actually true.

AB: I do too. But you're already on the Internet. There are so many distractions. If the computer is in front of you and you get an email, suddenly you're not watching the thing you were watching anymore, or someone Skypes you, or there's a website you wanted to check out. It's way easier to get distracted than when you're watching a television show. It's up to you to grab hold of the audience's attention in any medium.

PD: What other advice would you give to writers about how to get people to look at these ten-minute shows and how to create something that suits this medium?

AB: The most difficult part for me was getting the concept across in what would normally be an hour in a television show where you could lay all the elements on the table. With this you have ten minutes, so what mechanism do you have when you also don't have the budget for some things. Your only option is to hook them on story, hook them on the characters.

That becomes a vital piece when you're casting. If you can't afford people or you don't have the relationships to bring people in that are going to create that investment for you. There's only so much your words can do when you have that amount of time. You have to write faster but they also have to "act faster." They have to get their charisma across in a much more dramatic way than you would need to otherwise when you have time to live with the characters and fall in love with them. On the web, if you don't fall in love with them in the first five minutes, the series is done.

Fortunately, that's where my experience working in television was helpful because I could call people who I knew could do that. Are people going to fall in love with these characters and the situation they find themselves in? If so, we've got them.

PD: Let's talk about the show itself, *Caper*.

AB: *Caper* is about a team of superheroes who turn to a life of crime to make a living. The economy has been bad for everyone. When you get paid in compliments and keys to the city, how are you going to pay the rent? These guys are faced with very human concerns. It's a way of doing the superhero genre that makes the characters relatable. You can connect with them because they're going through the same struggles you are.

PD: Did you plan a one-season arc? A multiple season arc?

AB: We planned a one-season arc because you don't know if you're going to have more than that. Another thing about a web series is there is no pilot. The pilot is the first season. That's good because you can see everything unfold before any decision is made as to whether it's worthy of being picked up for more of the series. You're actually making a show; you're not just making a sample episode of a show. With a 90-minute season it works out to be like a TV movie.

PD: Would all 90 minutes work as a movie?

AB: It doesn't really play as a whole piece in that sense because we're trying to attract people on a weekly basis. You kind of have to re-up the idea of the show. We do it in a way that we don't have to say the words "previously on" but we have a narrative device that reminds you who these people are and what the show is about. The individual episodes are designed to be individual episodes.

PD: Where do you go from here? The show goes up. How are you going to tell people to watch?

AB: I could have done this show by myself. I could have financed it, distributed it online. But me posting something on the Internet is the same as any other person posting on the Internet. But Felicia Day has Geek & Sundry. She has a distribution model and publicity already in place.

PD: How many viewers does she have?

AB: I don't know. At least high six figures on a regular basis.

PD: When I've spoken to other digital series creators (who are not Netflix) I've heard numbers that are pretty small. Someone I spoke with said he made a pilot for $40,000 by getting everybody to work for free, raised his money on Kickstarter, and for all of that, his total viewership was around 36,000.

AB: That was the risk I wasn't willing to take. I'm well established in the geek community but I don't have a name that's going to attract viewers for my name alone. I'm not a selling point; Felicia is a selling point. If I'm going to invest my time and money I want to be sure there's going to be eyes on the first episode. It's my job to make sure the eyes stick around. I'm hoping with her network we will get eyes on that first episode.

I can't make this show for a second season on the same model as the first season. The hope is someone will want to invest. It will be airing on both YouTube and Hulu and they do ads on both. Google could invest more in YouTube if they want it to be the "new television." They're far away from doing that.

PD: We don't yet know what shape the future is going to take. What you're doing sounds like quality stuff, and that usually costs.

AB: I don't know how to make things on a budget. I'm paying my cast and crew $100 a day — everyone gets the same amount of money for the same amount of days — but their investment is not in the project as much as it is in me. It makes me feel good. Our regulars are regulars on television series and our guest stars are leads on other TV shows. The investment is in what could happen, not the thing that's here and now. That's my investment too — it's in the model and my ability to present something that will tell people there's something more here than what they've been seeing.

PD: Is your hope that *Caper* gets picked up by a cable channel, for example, and moves to regular television, or are you not even interested in that?

AB: There's more to *Caper*. There's more story to tell and I would love to tell it. If a studio wanted to come in and sweep us off our feet and put us on television or make a movie out of the concept we would not be averse to that. My fear is the lack of control that would result. That would be the antithesis of why I got into this in the first place.

PD: What does this bode for individual writers or writer-producers in the future?

AB: I think it bodes well. It's all about making things. No one is going to get a foothold in the new model if they don't take the risk and put themselves out there. The tough thing is what's it going to take to get people to notice you? That's always going to be the problem. I'm an established television writer and I still occasionally have that problem getting in the door at studios and networks because that's the business. There are only so many people they can see.

But if you're able to make something that people want to invest their time in, the creators need to figure out what that model is. We need to present it and then everybody has to catch up to us. That's the reason I'm doing this. I want to be a part of making that model. I don't want to be the one behind saying, oh, that's what's happening now? Okay, I guess I'm going to go pitch there. I want to be the one who dictates what people want to watch by making good things, not by making things a studio or network executive think is the future.

It's up to all the creators to step out of their comfort zone and make quality. I just want to be part of it.

JANE ESPENSON AND BRADLEY C. BELL

Like Amy Berg, Jane Espenson arrived online as an experienced television producer. But this is a tale of an odd couple, interviewed at a delightful lunch, as they sometimes completed each other's sentences.

With credits on *Buffy the Vampire Slayer, Battlestar Galactica*, and many other shows, Espenson was (and still is) an executive producer on broadcast series. At the same time, 20-something Bradley C. Bell was making YouTube videos starring himself as "Cheeks," a snarky, exhibitionistic, attention-craving Hollywood wannabe, whose persona was "as apt to make a dance video as give an assessment of Lindsay Lohan's courtroom body language," according to *Written By* magazine.

Espenson was interested in exploring comedy when she came upon Bell's audacious YouTube performance. Together, they developed *Husbands* about two gay men who drunk-marry. Funny thing is that the episodes that emerged on CW Seed (the digital series component of the CW) aren't really experimental; they're more like 20th-century sitcoms. That's intentional. Both assert they're making "online television," and shun the "web series" label. In fact, Bell embraces the historical context. He told *Written By* that he was thinking about *I Love Lucy*, "And then all of a sudden I thought, Oh my God, oh my God, newlyweds. Gay newlyweds, that's what this story is. Not a guy and his gal pal — that's *Will & Grace*, that was 15 years ago. What's the new version of that — it's *Mad About You* or *Bewitched*. With boys."

I asked if they want to be so traditional, why make it a digital series at all? Espenson explained, "We would have had to pitch to networks that would have changed it in the development process. Doing it this way allowed us to make exactly the product we wanted to make right away."

She continued, "In the first YouTube episodes we did of *Husbands* [before the show was picked up by CW Seed], we made sure each episode was

around two minutes because if people saw it was over three minutes they wouldn't bother watching. In Brad's YouTube videos, he edited out every breath between words so the minutes whipped by. It felt like they were paced for the modern attention span. They created a high energy field we wanted to capture with *Husbands*, and that was another reason to do the show in a nontraditional way."

Still, they relied on established sitcom structure. Bell said, "We made a pilot but we made sure each scene alone had a complication or some sort of twist or character revelation. Ideally, you're doing that in every scene anyway, but when you're doing something that's 22 minutes you might have a scene that could be cut but for us every single scene was *how are we going to get people to watch the next two minutes*."

Espenson amplified, "We did a total of four storylines, each equivalent to an episode of television. Season One was 11 two-minute episodes; Seasons Two, Three, and Four were eight-minute pieces that were like an act of ordinary television that could be stitched together into a 22-to-24-minute story."

"That was part of our philosophy," Bell interpolated, "that new media is not any different from television. There's still a question — if something works on the web and it moves over to traditional television, how is it reinterpreted? We believe it shouldn't have to change. It works on the web and it works as a broadcast episode."

Those comments brought our conversation to what I've been exploring in this book: What is the future of television? I knew Bell and Espenson had traveled to Google's Palo Alto campus to screen *Husbands* and gave a talk titled "Inventing Television: How *Husbands* Realizes the Promise." So I asked what television means to them.

Bell answered, "Television literally means far vision. When it was invented that meant taking a vision and transporting it across the room. Then it meant across country, and now it means across the world. The original notion of the inventor, Philo Farnsworth, was a world without war or poverty. He thought how could anyone be poor or harm someone else if we were able to connect with stories about each other's culture and history? It was a sort of utopia that Farnsworth envisioned with this technology.

"We're just seeing that realized with today's telecommunications media. To communicate you have to communicate on both sides. With standard television you can't communicate on both sides — you're shouting at people. The fallout of an industry that's been telling people what to think is that it's now facing feedback from the public."

Espenson concluded, "What we are seeing now on the Internet is the culmination of what television was meant to be."

THE TOP TIER

I wonder whether the arrival of powerful Old World showrunners in the digital New World will enhance its value and generate the respect digital series creators crave, or will they plow over the small start-ups? In 19th-century America, when tycoons ventured from East Coast industries to what had been the Wild West, the early wave of homesteading pioneers were pushed off their formerly free land when it was commandeered or procured for prices they couldn't afford. But online, space is theoretically infinite. Can Bambi coexist here with Godzilla? And what if Godzilla is an artist at heart?

Just because someone has been successful in the mainstream doesn't mean he or she lacks insight, talent, and the courage to try something new. It's as wrong to stereotype all big-league producers as barriers to creativity (though some may be) as it is wrong to stereotype all web series creators as amateurs (though some may be). Case in point: Jon Avnet (*Black Swan*, *Risky Business*, *Fried Green Tomatoes*) and Rodrigo Garcia (*In Treatment*). Together they created WIGS, a high-quality web channel that boasts the kind of writers, directors, and actors that would interest a premium cable network.

Garcia said, "We're old fuddy-duddies as far as the Internet's concerned, but you don't have to read the crystal ball to know that the Internet is here to stay. But storytelling is not going to go anywhere. We wanted to tell [stories] on the Internet in a valuable way."

In the *Los Angeles Times*, Dawn Chmielewski and Yvonne Villarreal reported, "Avnet and Garcia say they are in it for the long haul, thanks to backing from a big-name advertiser, American Express, and a television network, Fox, which views the channel as a way to inexpensively test dramatic concepts that could reach the television screen. Avnet, Garcia, and their Hollywood collaborators are eager to learn the nuances of storytelling in a medium that rewards brevity, rapid pacing, and near-immediate plot reveals — and do so without creating second-class, tiny-screen entertainment."

With a $5 million initial advance from YouTube to create 100 episodes of original scripted programming for and about women, it launched 18 series in its first two years and amassed 200,000 subscribers, generating an aggregate of around 46 million views. Their template involves episodes eight to nine minutes long, each ending with a cliff-hanger. "We challenged ourselves from the beginning that every episode, no matter how short, had to have an impact and had to push the story forward," Garcia explained. With that impetus, they produced the equivalent of six feature-length movies the first year, an unheard-of pace in traditional media.

Viewer attention has gone to *Susanna*, a 12-part series starring *True Blood*'s Anna Paquin as a new mother who develops acute postpartum depression. Paquin commented, "This whole platform for female-driven narratives and storytelling is just really exciting. As a woman, it's sometimes a little hard to find material that's challenging or interesting, where you're not playing a wife or a girlfriend. ...That's why I wanted to be a part of it."

Blue, about a mother with a secret life, starring Julia Stiles, has also established a fan base. Stiles observed, "A couple of times, people have actually confused it with a TV show — 'Oh, I miss that show you're on.' People so often are watching any kind of programming on their computers, the line between traditional TV and the Internet is so blurred."

If the boundary between traditional and online television is blurry on the near side, the boundary on the far frontier is disintegrating altogether. Beyond defined series (whether network or web) lies a porous landscape of interactivity and "transmedia" that I'll discuss in the next chapter.

Some of the makers are the same executives who prevailed in the Old World, though. Anthony Zuiker created the original *CSI* series still accruing large ratings on CBS after many years. You could hardly find more mainstream television. This predictable procedural spawned spin-off shows, each of which uses the same model of clue-chasing stories that solve crimes within one hour. Yet here he is creating *Cybergeddon*, an original digital series on Yahoo about an international cyber-crime ring. The franchise sounds familiar — more crime chasing — but Zuiker said he believes the format represents the future of storytelling, as nine ten-minute web-only installments that build to a 90-minute movie.

"The relationship between Silicon Valley and Hollywood needs to be figured out — and figured out fast," Zuiker told Dawn Chmielewski in the *Los Angeles Times*. For example, as a companion to the episodes, Zuiker developed what he calls "zips," one-minute clips that explore the characters' backstories in ways that inform the narrative.

Zuiker continued in the *Times*, "You can watch these zips, binge and binge and binge on narrative stories that are shot at the same level as the movie. It'll draw you into the movie. These are little PR soldiers. They can live all over cyberspace."

For all the exploration, the business side is familiar. Norton, the antivirus software company, not only sponsored the show but participated fully in marketing, promoting *Cybergeddon* on boxes of its software and employing the alerts typically reserved to warn a user of a virus.

So have we come full circle to the time when advertisers owned and controlled shows in the early days of television? Are we really exploring new worlds where no one has gone before? Or are we just populating the New World with all the old ways?

INTERACT WITH CHAPTER SEVEN

- Create four different interpretations of one show by adapting it for specific platforms: (1) traditional network (2) cable (3) premium online and (4) web series. Pay attention to changes in length, characterization, intricacy, style, budget, and choice of subjects as you change platforms.
- Take a feature-length screenplay (your original or any movie script) and divide it into episodes for YouTube. Each episode should be around eight to ten minutes long. Make a "season" of 12 episodes that adds to around two hours. Now check the episodes to see if these breaks really work. They probably won't because they lack cliff-hangers. Go back through and reshape the episodes for digital viewing.
- Find the highest rated original scripted series on YouTube. What are the qualities that make it so popular?

CHAPTER EIGHT

THE FAR FRONTIER

INTERACTIVE TELEVISION ISN'T NEW. Way back in the 1950s *Winky Dink and You* (on CBS) involved viewers in storytelling, pioneering interactive programming at the same time television itself was pioneered. Children sent away for a kit that had crayons and a plastic screen that stuck to the TV tube with static electricity. When a character needed help, children would be asked to get him out of trouble by drawing on the screen. For example, if he needed to cross a river that had no bridge, the viewer would draw a line so he could escape. The grownup host encouraged kids to invite a friend over to watch the program; sharing the experience was essential to it. So helping Winky Dink in his adventures became an early expression of "participation television." We'll get to what that means.

Unlike theatrical movies, the very nature of television has always involved audiences on an intimate level in a personal space, while at the same time creating a virtual community beyond geographic bounds. Those characteristics account for TV's continuing power as much as the quality of the shows; that's why television transcends any particular device on which shows are watched. None of that is new.

But now, interactivity is positioned on the frontier. This is beyond what I discussed in the section about Amazon Studios' crowd-sourced script development. In the Amazon model, individual writers commented on and contributed to another writer's pilot. That's a limited kind of interactivity targeted at affecting someone else's project. A second model of interactivity is fan fiction that predates television, in which audiences who love characters in a book, play, movie, or TV show imagine further adventures for them. But now this is different. The next step in interactivity minimizes the individual sense of ownership, replacing it with what some describe as a "democratic" creative process, and others describe as anarchy. Some call it the "hive mind."

"The hive mind" comes from an idea that all humans are one entity, like a beehive or an ant colony, and that our inventions that make us proud of ourselves are really the products of group consciousness. Everyone plays his or her part as an individual, and is important in that sense like an individual ant or bee, but in the big picture no individual matters. Or each of us matters to the extent we are unique aspects of the whole, but on our own, no hive, colony, or culture could exist. An example often cited is guessing how many tiny items are in a jar. Experiments have shown that no individual guesses the correct number. But, with a large enough number of participants, averaging everyone's guess always results in an accurate count.

Can we behave like bees or ants? Should we if we can? Proponents of making art collectively don't address that. The arguments, instead, are that more interesting products emerge when more voices are heard; and it's the wave of the future, like it or not. A generation sharing openly on social media and willingly surrendering privacy online will demand participation in its entertainment on every level.

That's the philosophical basis for *hitRECord*, a series that premiered on Pivot-TV in 2014 before moving onto YouTube and iTunes. Executive Producer Joseph Gordon-Levitt, who starred in the NBC sitcom *3rd Rock from the Sun*, told the *Los Angeles Times* that the underlying site (hitrecord.org) encourages participants to build on one another's work — "remixing" — to create content through vignettes harvested by his company. "If you go back to early human beings," he said, "the origin of people telling stories or singing songs or painting images was probably quite communal and collaborative."

The first episode features the work of 426 contributors pieced together by a staff of a dozen or so editors who sifted through the hundreds of offerings that ranged from photos to film clips to music to personal stories.

One story submitted from Scotland was by a woman with night blindness who spoke of seeing stars for the first time. "That's a story where if I hired a roomful of writers here in town and said, 'Okay, write me a good short film about somebody's first time doing something,' I wouldn't have gotten something so profound," Gordon-Levitt declared. This kind of belief in the open-collaboration process leads him and his supporters to see themselves as redefining television by being agents of change.

Not everyone agrees. The *New York Times*' Jon Caramanica described *hitRECord* as a "vanity project masking as generosity."

STORY-WORLDING

"Go where your audience lives" is a credo of Participation Continuum run by Brian Seth Hurst who is an ardent advocate of "story-worlding." As CEO of The Opportunity Management Company, who also served on the boards of the Television Academy and the Producers Guild of America, Hurst consults on the collaboration between the storyteller and the audience. Mostly, he deals with businesses, but I asked him about the creator's role in the future of television.

BRIAN SETH HURST

BRIAN SETH HURST: If you create a really great story world, the audience is going to take over that story world. They want to be a part of it. This is a generational thing. Millennials are much more inclined to do this than baby boomers or even Gen-Xers. They want to feel they have some ownership over the story and something at stake.

The truth is you're not going to have the control you used to have either as an author or as an auteur or as a showrunner. If you've done your job correctly and defined your world with characters and a great mythology behind it, the audience is going to want to be a part of that. That conversation between the storyteller and the audience is a tricky thing especially now that we're entering the era of collective collaboration. Though this may not have a direct influence on network or cable television right now, I believe it will in the future.

You can look at the audience as co-marketers right now because they have a job to do. If they really love your show it doesn't matter what you try to do on Twitter or Facebook or any social media; if the audience loves your show and there's an authenticity to what you're doing, they do all that marketing for you. In Season One if you create a great show, you'll know by episode 3 or 4 because the community will activate around it, they will share it and turn it into a hit. But then the storyteller becomes answerable to them. The idea of the storyteller being more sensitive to the audience but then not compromising is a fine line they're going to walk.

PAMELA DOUGLAS: From the point of view of a writer, how would it change the process of writing? The idea of interactivity has been around for years ever since movie theaters tried those buttons on the seats where the majority of the theater audience could choose the ending. At that time, Steve Martin commented they're paying me a million dollars to write this movie; why should some schmuck be able to change my ending?

BSH: I think the writer's responsibility is to maintain the integrity of the story world they've created. The idea of creating the really solid story world with solid characters — all the elements of good storytelling — that doesn't change. You can't impose interactivity on something. That's why the buttons on theater seats didn't work. We come to identify with a story in some manner — we'll identify with a character, or it might be aspirational, something we want. The idea is that you've created a story world and you're responsible for maintaining its integrity. Someone has to maintain the vision and it doesn't matter if the vision is altered by the viewers because the community itself will moderate what that story world is. If you've defined a story world really well then people can live in it.

You asked how this changes for the writer. The storytelling elements don't change. It doesn't matter what happens; the elements don't change. But you can't impose your idea of interactivity on top of a story. That's why I'm a fan of watching the audience in the first six episodes. Then I would look to the Net and see the conversations. I would keep those conversations as a playground on which things can happen. I would catch the trend and make it easier for that to happen within my domain. I would formalize the audience behavior so they could do it within my world and find a way to monetize that. It's a combination of observation and storytelling.

PD: Starting at the beginning of the creation of a show, before you have a fan base, coming to the "big bang" of a show, in your perspective, what would you have a writer make? What would a writer create before there is an audience in order to maximize the kind of potential for interaction you're talking about?

BSH: I'm a storyteller myself so the only thing I can say is tell the story you want to tell. Be the craftsman. Know what the story world is. I don't think those things change. Don't think "let me put interactivity in here." That's not it. Give the audience a chance to identify with the things you create.

If your audience is invested in a show they start to tweet that they want John and Jane to be together. You can see that in the data. So the showrunner can look at the data and decide what to do with it. He might say okay, we're going to put these characters together because that's what the audience wants. But I'm only going to put them together for a little while, and then I'm going to kill one of them off. That doesn't piss off the audience. It actually works. You give them what they want and they understand that from their linear writing. But a good storyteller is not going to completely sell himself out to what the audience wants.

If you look at the next generation, the millennials, this is their life. They've never not known interactive storytelling. They're all storytellers on their own, whether they're using Facebook or Tumblr.

PD: Where does that leave professional writers?

BSH: You still have to have someone who knows what they're doing and who is the visionary for the story world and can create those characters and story arcs and maintain the integrity of the story world. The one thing that doesn't change is great story. Great characters. That will always be the same.

I think this is a great time of opportunity for writers. And it's incumbent upon writers, besides learning their craft, to understand how technology enables the conversation between them and their audience.

T BONE'S RESPONSE

Since we're "interacting," I'll share an alternate perspective. In a 2013 Q&A with Chris Willman in *The Hollywood Reporter*, T Bone Burnett let loose on the so-called digital revolution. Though the award-winning music producer refers mostly to the music industry, these excerpts reflect an attitude towards crowd-power that is also shared by many producers of television.

"The worldwide web was supposed to give everybody access and democratize everything. It was supposed to create a level field and increase the middle class and everybody had more access and more information. But now anybody can say anything and nobody cares. This is the problem of ubiquitous data.

"And what's happened in reality is that the power's been consolidated in very, very few companies, and the middle class of musicians really has just been wiped out. I mean the Internet has been an honest-to-God con.

"The Internet went into: 'Everything wants to be free, give your stuff away, pass it around, we don't care about the definitive version — the hive mind will take care of it. Leave it to the wisdom of the crowd, that'll work it all out, and everything will be fine in the end.'

"The car industry gets decimated and people go into apoplexy. The recording industry gets destroyed and people seem to be sanguine or happy about it, almost, because they're getting everything for free. If somebody had come down from Silicon Valley 30 years ago and said 'I've got this new technology, and you're gonna be able to see all around the world, transfer your stuff all over the world, you're gonna be able to send things, you'll be able to see your friends, you'll be able to hear music — all you have to do is give up your privacy and your royalties,' everybody would have said, 'Get the f— out of town! Right now! Get out of here!' Instead, these guys came down with their shtick, and everybody went, 'Well, how can we make money from this great new technology?' 'Oh, you're not gonna make *money* from it. Everything's gonna be free. Just give us the intellectual property we can send around in our pipes, everybody will subscribe, and then we'll be rich. Not *you*, though.' [*Laughs.*] 'Don't ask us what we're doing with the money. Just make the stuff and send it to us for free.' That's how much of a straight-up con it's been. People in Hollywood, we should go up there with pitchforks and torches to Silicon Valley now. Unfortunately, that's [how sophisticated] our response would be — pitchforks and torches.

"Promoting yourself and crowd-funding and all that kind of stuff, that's no way for an artist to live. When I go to one of these conferences and people ask me 'How do I market myself on the Internet?' and all that kind of stuff: Look, your *fans* will market you on the Internet. But if you want to be a musician, practice eight hours a day. I don't believe in crowd-sourcing because you'll end up doing the same thing over and over again. People tend to want artists to do the same thing, and it is incumbent upon artists to do something that the audience doesn't want — yet. I'll tell you this. I won't follow an artist who will be led by his audience. Because I don't want to have to follow an artist that I have to lead."

TRANSMEDIA

On the far side of interactive television, beyond the whirlpools of artists who are led by crowds, lies the land of transmedia. It's on the same frontier of the New World as interactivity, where natural resources (its stories) are spread around, rather than being vaulted in the castles of the Old World, or sold to an elite who can afford them as in premium cable, or are personal experiments and expressions, as in web series. Transmedia, our last stop on this journey, aims to transcend.

What does that mean? I asked Jay Bushman, who has two Emmy Awards, the first two ever given for original interactive content, both for his role as a transmedia producer. In 2013 the award went to *The Lizzie Bennet Diaries* that had 100 episodes, each around five or six minutes long, on a main YouTube channel, and also 150 shorter episodes across five different channels, and an uncounted number of tweets, posts, and other communications that were intrinsic to the series.

But let me back up to meeting him because it reveals something about who is out there on the edge. A current student in one of my writing classes, who is 22, mentioned that she had a part-time job as a transmedia editor. I asked for an introduction to the guy she was working for. So he and I arranged to meet at a local café. There I was scanning the room for what I assumed would be, essentially, a male version of my very young student. Or maybe he'd be someone with tattoos and piercings and a shaved head, or dreadlocks. I waited and waited. Did he ditch the interview? Finally I realized that only one other person was here alone: a man with graying hair. That was Jay Bushman. So much for stereotypes.

I asked him what is transmedia, and he answered…

JAY BUSHMAN

JAY BUSHMAN: We have a joke that you put two transmedia creators in a room and pretty soon you'll have three definitions of transmedia.

One branch is rooted in franchises. That's most of what you see in the press — you have movies, and video games that tie into that, and books, and it's all part of the same story world. But we already had a word for that: continuity.

You see the Marvel example: You have the *Iron Man 3* movie, *The Shield* TV show, the comic books. But each piece of that is a discrete entity. You can watch the *Iron Man* movie and not have watched *Thor*; *Iron Man 3* is an entity unto itself. You can watch *The Shield* series and each episode is a story unto itself.

I approach transmedia from a different perspective. I use multiple channels, multiple formats, multiple media, and have each piece part of a larger whole but none of the individual pieces stands alone. So it becomes a multimedia experience where you get part of the story here but you have to switch to another place to get another part. By putting all those individual pieces together you create something larger than the whole. It's a singular experience.

That's still trying to find its feet as a repeatable model. It's difficult. People get used to consuming media in one way. There's a whole culture built around making television shows or making comic books. But when you try to make a single story that uses all these elements where you have to cross from looking at something on your website to looking at something on your phone or Twitter to get a single experience it can be challenging to frame that, challenging to sell that, really challenging to make money on that.

PAMELA DOUGLAS: It's also challenging for the player or audience to be on all those things at once.

JB: There are three different levels of audiences: the people who would hunt out everything, the people who would follow along and watch the people who would hunt out everything, and the people who would dip in and out. The challenge was to make something that these three segments of the audience could consume simultaneously.

I've taken those ideas and tried to apply them to making dramatic fictional series. In *Lizzie Bennet Diaries* everything is scripted. It's a ton of work. It's hard for people to grasp when most of the content on YouTube is vaudeville-like personality-driven short joke type of thing. There's a lot of scripted entertainment on YouTube but it's still in its infancy.

Lizzie Bennet Diaries is an amalgam of all these ideas I've been playing with for a long time — how to make one cohesive story that takes place on YouTube and on your Twitter feed and on your social media feeds and place it in the world. We scripted all that too.

Early on, as my price for being on the show, I needed to be a member of the writing staff and sit in the writers' room with everyone else to break stories and make decisions at that level so the transmedia elements would be tied in tightly to everything else.

Traditionally what happens on network shows and every other show is they write the show and bring in another team to do what they call ancillary material. There are two conflicting paradigms here. One is that you have your core creative team and bring in specialists to do this other stuff. But what have we been taught from the very beginning as writers? If it's not essential, cut it. So what happens when you bring in other people to bolt on other stuff that is not essential? Because it's not essential, it's not enjoyable, it's not fun, and it's treated as ancillary content, which means it's not important. The big crusade for me is to get this material elevated past the level of ancillary, to be tied into the world in a larger sense.

PD: Are you a writer? Is that how you consider yourself?

JB: I am a writer. I started writing stage plays and screenplays; I went to film school at University of North Carolina, Greensboro. I graduated in the mid-90s. It was the last gasp of shooting on film and putting everything on your credit cards. I ended up with credit card debt and short films on 16mm. So I transitioned into writing.

This is around the time an explosion was happening on the Internet among people who were using free and cheaply available services to make content directly for their audiences, bypassing gatekeepers. The movement asked: How do you use the Internet to connect directly with your audience? But how do you do it as a dramatist? You can't just upload a script. A script isn't an experience; it's an instruction set on how to make an experience. How do you create an experience online directly for your audience? That's when I went back to my history with alternate reality games. I said you could use their techniques as a storytelling tool. How do you use the web to tell a story?

I got involved in real-time storytelling, using social media. In 2008, I got an idea from a couple of guys who restaged *War of the Worlds* on Twitter. They created an outline of a script. It said, for example, at seven p.m. you see lights in the sky… at one a.m. the tripods come out. Now you use your Twitter accounts to tell us what you are seeing. What does it mean to you? What is your personal story of *War of the Worlds*? It was so much fun and eye-opening to see how you could make these giant collaborative story worlds and let people play around in them. I felt we found something powerful so I started experimenting with that model. I did a few of these fun experiments and they taught me how you can create a world environment and invite people in to be a part of it and tell stories within it.

PD: This group world-building sounds like fun. But writers tend to want to express their vision with stories that build to a certain end. I'm sure Vince Gilligan would not have wanted someone else to change the ending of *Breaking Bad*. How do you put those together?

JB: When people start talking about interactive content they leap to "choose your own adventure" user-generated content, giving up story control to the audience. I don't believe in that. One of the tenets we talked about was "*Hamlet* isn't a better play if you let the audience choose the ending." Go to your bookshelf at home and look at all the books you own, and count how many of them are "choose your own adventures." The answer is going to be zero because "choose your own adventure" is not going to be emotionally satisfying. When multiple endings are possible, no individual ending is important.

We were looking for ways to use this interactive conduit but still be able to tell emotionally engaging stories. I developed a working theory based in part upon thinking done by others. There is a continuum. On one end is the three-act structure based on Aristotelian philosophy, with a diagram of tension we've all seen. At the other end of the spectrum is The

Magic Circle. This is game storytelling like *World of Warcraft*. The game creators make a universe with rules and stories, but the audience experiences things in their own time, their own way, and everyone has a different experience within this world. The storyteller's basic job in this paradigm is to define what's inside the circle, and what's outside. Everything inside the circle is the story; everything outside the circle is not.

I looked at this continuum, and asked what if we put the two ends together. I started working with an idea I call Through-Line and Magic Circle. You have a story world, an environment, and in the middle of this world is a through-line story, an anchor story that doesn't change. To my mind Magic Circle stories only become emotionally engaging if they have a through-line to play off.

That's the model *Lizzie Bennet Diaries* is built on. We have a through-line — the story of *Pride and Prejudice*, the story of Lizzie Bennet and her sisters and Mr. Darcy and how they come together. But around that story we have created a world and invited the fans in to play little parts in this surrounding world. The characters can converse with this audience, and it makes this story world real, immediate, and continuous.

We told that story over the span of an entire year with two video episodes per week at minimum, but social media and transmedia content was three, four times a week or more. That created a world that was always there to the audience. You could be out doing something else, pick up your phone and oh, look, there's Lizzie tweeting about something. The characters were always available to the viewer. No matter what time of day, something was going on. If you missed something today, you could catch it tomorrow, and things kept going while you missed it. It had a lived-in feel. That's the power. It gives the audience a sense of ownership of the world and these characters.

In order to get to that you have to commit to this world-building. A lot of stuff that gets done by network and cable shows functions like one-offs. For example, *Breaking Bad* created a website for Sol, the lawyer. But that's a one-time joke — you look at it and go Ha, and the experience is over. But we created a world where each piece leads to something else. It's a world to live in, not just a one-off tactic to provoke a response. The response we want is for you to engage in the story world.

PD: Having won two Emmys from the Television Academy for something that's not what people used to think of as television, though the Academy does, what is television?

JB: In defining transmedia, I look at television. Television simply means I can see something that's far away. But what it really means is this entire ecosystem that has grown up around the ability to do that. The walls are all breaking down. The convergence people have been talking about for 25 years is here finally. We're in this fertile period where we can make stuff and put it out. We'll figure out what the new paths are.

THE INTERACTIVE TELEVISION ALLIANCE

Hearing so many emerging possibilities made me want a vantage point with perspective on the whole frontier. The Interactive Television Alliance (ITA) is a nonprofit trade association that's been around since 2002. Its founders included Disney, Intel, Comcast, TiVo, all the set-top box people, Microsoft's Advanced Television, and they work horizontally across the various business organizations like the National Association of Broadcasters and cable television associations. They're not about the creative process, but they know the terrain. So I asked CEO Allison Dollar for her overview.

ALLISON DOLLAR

ALLISON DOLLAR: We all knew the locus of control was going to shift to the consumer, which has happened. That means methods of distribution are fundamentally altered. But we're still in the days of people focusing too much on the technology as the driver. I don't think it is. Technology is responsible for big shifts in consumer expectation. But the changes are only enabled by the technology. Technology had not been the driver.

PAMELA DOUGLAS: So what is the driver of change?

AD: The driver is a more fragmented distribution system. Once you open the door to saying, for instance, somebody's cat video is worth as many repeat viewers as a prime-time show, that's going to be affecting economics. So even if things are ephemeral it doesn't really matter because when you end up having enough of them that are big enough, larger players come in, and you become the next generation worth distribution. That drives the whole chain. That's why YouTube has Makers Studios here; Amazon has its own studios now. That has upended things in an odd way because they're really not doing anything new. They're just becoming the newer big players.

But one major difference on the business side is to be looking at the very front end of a creative process. The front end is where the sponsorship hooks are going to be.

PD: What does "front end" mean?

AD: It's the creative process as a writer or producer. The front end is the conceptual stage. That's where the studios used to be for many years. What are the product tie-ins, what are the brand tie-ins? Clearly, what matters is storytelling, narrative.

But with technology, we're going to a bit of a plateau. The most important piece is the cloud delivery, not the gadgets, the idea you can decentralize certain forms of distribution in ways you couldn't do easily before. That's made a real difference in how fast things can go to market and catch on due to buzz. It ends up creating new content that can be packaged.

I think the pie just gets bigger and bigger. If you look at video consumption, video has grown overall. The number of gadgets we own continues to grow. In terms of money, we do see some budgets shifting more to online platforms. But there's also more money being spent on advertising as well.

Some huge and amazing stories can come out of the co-creation process, engaging fans as they are in the fan fiction world. And surprising things are sometimes made by thousands of people around the globe collaborating on a project. I do think that's a huge growth area. But I don't think the new structures are going to fundamentally replace the essentials. It doesn't mean our traditional narrative structures go away, or that forms of building character, or intentions, or resolving dramatic tension is going away anytime soon.

Television is still an aspirational business. So if you are the creators of *The Annoying Orange* and you get a huge following on YouTube, and then you get your deal with Comedy Central, there's a trajectory of a success path that has not dissipated yet.

PD: What advice would you give a writer-producer who is interested in creating original television in the future?

AD: I would advise screenwriters to be aware of the large market forces, the various choices of paths of distribution partners, and how that impacts whether you close a deal. It's probably smart to be a little more versed than you had to be in previous times about how the business works as a business. It's better for you if you have some notion as your own advocate as a professional about what the big forces are in the business now.

MICKEY MOUSE

I began this chapter talking about the 1950s, and I'll "bookend" it referring to the 1950s again with the quintessential transmedia character: Mickey Mouse. He'd already been around as a cartoon for decades by the time Disneyland opened in 1955; in the years since *Steamboat Willie* (in 1928), Mickey appeared in movies such as *Fantasia* (1940), in animated TV series, and on merchandise and games. But in 1955, Mickey walked off the screen into Disneyland where a costumed performer interacted as a living being.

And that changed everything. Not that people hadn't dressed up as fantasy characters before — humans performed rituals dressed as animals for eons, and historical reenactments and role-playing have been common for a long time. But mutating an original screen creation to become a living interaction presaged a likely next evolution in entertainment.

Futurists speculate that "experience" will be the new watchword. Places formerly known as theme parks will be rebranded "experience parks." Virtual reality and holograms will move characters off the screen into your room where you will seem to inhabit the space where a scene plays out. That could cause a new definition of "off screen" and impact how much is written for action that is now out of frame or in a background.

What matters here is not future tech. This is about going beyond platforms so that human beings are in touch with other humans. It's a different way to think about the "hive." We don't do well in isolation. Probably when early humans became separated from the group they were eaten, and we never forgot how bad that felt. Unfortunately, new media has the ability to separate us into units staring into personal screens — all the people meeting for lunch, looking at their phones instead of each other. So now we're in the throes of a push-back through mass "friending" and frantic connections on social media. But that's not enough. As a species we seem to need to touch each other, to know each other in more than 140 characters.

And that brings us full circle to storytelling, and to our conclusion…

INTERACT WITH CHAPTER EIGHT

- Imagine an interactive component of an existing show that doesn't yet have one. This may include a game, shopping site, interface with a character, clues to a mystery, additional story lines or backstory.
- Plan a transmedia campaign that involves at least three different platforms. Examples might be: YouTube series + Twitter + phone; or cable series + interactive game + text messages; or video + Facebook + online contest. Be sure all content adds to a single narrative through-line.
- Think about the "hive mind" experiment where crowd-sourcing was able to guess the number of items in a jar though no individual succeeded. Why does that work? Hint: The answer is not a magical energy. Consider the science underlying the "bell curve."
- How can television encourage understanding across cultures in the future?

CONCLUSION

THE KEYS TO THE FUTURE are on your keyboard.

In a time of far-reaching change, the specific shows, even whole channels and the methods of distribution that I mentioned in this book will be different by the time you're reading this. The frontier will move, as it always does, and no matter how fast you travel, you will not exceed the speed of the light emanating from the television screens in the distance.

Everything I've shared with you, and the insights contributed by the many writers, producers, and executives interviewed, can be the basis for your continuing journey. To help with your future explorations, I'll post an occasional blog on my website: www.PamDouglasBooks.com.

But your own stories remain the ticket to ride. Your characters and their relationships will evolve, as will their challenges, fun, and fantasies. To the extent your stories are authentic, they will resonate with your audience, however you define an audience. Whether you see yourself as part of a collective global spirit or an individual creator, you are a voice in the most powerful communications medium on earth. You are a witness to the human condition. You are the one who forms a tale of these times.

The keys to the future of television are on your keyboard.

RESOURCES FOR YOU

Writers Guild of America, West
7000 West Third Street
Los Angeles, CA 90048
(323) 951-4000
www.wga.org

Intellectual Property Registry
(323) 782-4500
www.wgaregistry.org
James R. Webb Memorial Library
(323) 782-4544
Located on the first floor of the WGA. Open to the public to read scripts and view shows.

Writers Guild of America, East
555 West 57th Street
New York, NY 10019
(212) 767-7800
www.wgaeast.org
Writers Guilds affiliated with the WGA are located in many countries, for example the Writers' Guild of Great Britain and the New Zealand Writers Guild.

The Paley Center for Media (West)
465 N. Beverly Drive
Beverly Hills, CA 90210
(310) 786-1000
www.paleycenter.org
Reading and viewing is free and open to the public.

The Paley Center for Media (East)
25 W. 52nd Street
New York, NY
(212) 621-6600
www.paleycenter.org

Television Academy
5220 Lankershim Blvd.
North Hollywood, CA 91601
(818) 754-2800
www.emmys.com

RECOMMENDED READING

Douglas, Pamela. *Writing the TV Drama Series, Third Edition*. Studio City, CA: Michael Wiese Productions, 2011. (This is the essential companion to *The Future of Television*.)

Grisanti, Jennifer. *Story Line: Finding Gold in Your Life Story*. Studio City, CA: Michael Wiese Productions, 2011.

Kirschner, Carole. *Hollywood Game Plan*. Studio City, CA: Michael Wiese Productions, 2012.

Lotz, Amanda D. *The Television Will Be Revolutionized*. New York: NYU Press, 2007.

Pyle, Marx H. *Television on the Wild, Wild Web*. Studio City, CA: Michael Wiese Productions, 2014.

Sepinwall, Alan. *The Revolution Was Televised*. New York: Touchstone, 2013.

CREDITS

TEXT

p. 20 "TV Has Always Been a Work in Progress" by the Curators of the Paley Center for Media. *New York Times*, June 12, 2006. Reprinted with permission of The Paley Center.

p. 100 "Q & A with Beau Willimon" by Dina Gachman. *Studio System News*, June 12, 2013. Reprinted with permission of *Studio System News*.

p. 131 "Amazon's big TV push reflects reality of a swiftly changing business" by Robert Lloyd. *Los Angeles Times*, May 8, 2013. Copyright © *Los Angeles Times*. Reprinted with permission.

p. 190 "T Bone Burnett vs Silicon Valley" by Chris Willman. *The Hollywood Reporter*, October 31, 2013. Copyrighted 2014. Prometheus Global Media. 110018:514AT. Reprinted with permission.

IMAGES

Game of Thrones®, *True Detective*℠, and *Veep*® photographs photo courtesy HBO®.

p. 16 *Candorville*, October 22–23, 2013. Reprinted by permission of Bell Cartoons/Darrin Bell.

pp. 34, 54, 94–95 "The Old World," "Between Worlds," "The New World," original artwork by Raya Yarbrough, 2014.

ABOUT THE AUTHOR

PAMELA DOUGLAS is the author of *Writing the TV Drama Series*, now in its third edition (MWP 2011). The acclaimed book has been translated into several languages, and adopted by network mentoring programs at CBS and NBC. It is considered the premiere source on the subject.

She is an award-winning screenwriter, and was honored with the Humanitas Prize for *Between Mother and Daughter* (CBS) that also won nomination for a Writers Guild Award. Multiple Emmy nominations and awards from American Women in Radio and Television went to other shows she has written, and her credits include developing the series *Ghostwriter*, and writing for *Star Trek: the Next Generation*, and many others.

At the University of Southern California, she is a tenured professor in the School of Cinematic Arts, where she teaches writing for television. She has also been a member of the Board of Directors of the Writers Guild of America, West.

She consults internationally to professional TV writers and producers, and has lectured in Africa, Europe, and throughout the United States.

Further information is available at: www.PamDouglasBooks.com, and she can be contacted at pamdouglaswords@aol.com.

WRITING THE TV DRAMA SERIES 3RD EDITION

HOW TO SUCCEED AS A PROFESSIONAL WRITER IN TV

PAMELA DOUGLAS

This new edition builds on the book's reputation by bringing the very latest information, insights, and advice from major writers and producers. It is a complete resource for anyone who wants to write and produce for a television drama series or create an original series, as well as for teachers in screenwriting classes and workshops. Offering practical industry information and artistic encouragement, the book is both nuts-and-bolts and inspiration. The Third Edition leads readers into the future and engages provocative issues about the interface between traditional TV and emerging technologies and endless possibilities.

"Right now is the golden age of TV drama and Pamela Douglas' Writing the TV Drama Series *is far and away the best resource I know of for any writer wishing to work in this tremendously challenging and rewarding field."*

– Daniel Petrie, Jr., president, Writers Guild of America, West
and Oscar-nominated writer

"Remarkably comprehensive and up-to-date, Writing the TV Drama Series *is a candid, enthusiastic introduction to the craft and culture of dramatic television."*

– Jeff Melvoin, executive producer, *Alias*, *Northern Exposure*

"The breadth and depth of practical advice on real-world writing should enlighten and inspire any aspiring TV drama writer. It should enlighten because it is clear, free of jargon and explains the business and the design of television dramas. The interviews with successful writers makes this book valuable all by themselves, but there's so much more."

– Diane Carson, Ph.D., editorial VP of University Film & Video Association

PAMELA DOUGLAS is an award-winning screenwriter with numerous credits in television drama. She was honored with the Humanitas Prize and won nominations for Writers Guild Awards and Emmys. Twice her shows also won awards from American Women in Radio and Television. As a developer, she wrote the pilot, bible, and 13 episodes of the acclaimed series *Ghostwriter*. Additional series credits include *Star Trek: The Next Generation*, *Frank's Place*, *Paradise*, *Trapper John, M.D.*, and many others. She has been a member of the Board of Directors of the Writers Guild of America. At the University of Southern California, she is a tenured professor in the School of Cinematic Arts, where she is head of the Television Track in the Screenwriting Division.

$26.95 · 250 PAGES · ORDER NUMBER 172RLS · ISBN: 9781615930586

24 HOURS | 1.800.833.5738 | WWW.MWP.COM

CHANGE YOUR STORY, CHANGE YOUR LIFE
A PATH TO SUCCESS

JEN GRISANTI

Divorce. Job loss. Illness. The death of a loved one. What does one do after experiencing any of life's major turning points? *Change Your Story, Change Your Life* tackles that question and more, showing readers how to become the hero of their own stories and change the direction of their lives. After working as a Hollywood story analyst for more than 20 years, 12 of them as a studio executive, Jen Grisanti provides readers with the story tools necessary to "write their story" the way they wish it to be – and to "change their life" in the process.

Author, consultant, and international speaker Jen Grisanti instructs readers on how to apply story tools to their own lives, illuminating how everyone can become the hero of their own story. Based on her own experiences dealing with major life changes and developing methods with which to turn negative experiences into positive ones, Grisanti is a skilled guide in teaching readers how to live new life stories of their own making.

"Reading this wise, insightful, and inspirational book not only helped my writing, it helped me deal with difficult life issues. If it's true that writing is the best therapy, then this is the therapist we all need."

– Pamela Wallace, screenwriter; producer; Academy Award-winning co-writer of *Witness*

"Every writer knows that rewriting is infinitely easier than pounding out the first draft. Now in this brilliant book, Jen Grisanti shows us how we can apply the same principles to our own lives, taking a first pass that never quite comes together and turning it into everything we've ever wanted it to be."

– William Rabkin, Executive Producer: *Diagnosis Murder*; author: *Writing The Pilot*; Professor of Screenwriting, UC Riverside-Palm Desert

International speaker JEN GRISANTI is an acclaimed Story/Career Consultant at Jen Grisanti Consultancy, Inc. Grisanti is also a Writing Instructor for Writers on the Verge at NBC, a former studio executive, a blogger for *The Huffington Post*, and author of *Story Line: Finding Gold In Your Life Story* and *TV Writing Tool Kit: How To Write a Script That Sells.*

$16.95 · 145 PAGES · ORDER # CHANGE · ISBN: 9781611250176

STORY LINE

FINDING GOLD IN YOUR LIFE STORY

JEN GRISANTI

Story Line: Finding Gold in Your Life Story is a practical and spiritual guide to drawing upon your own story and fictionalizing it into your writing. As a Story Consultant and former VP of Current Programs at CBS/Paramount, most of the author's work with writers has focused on creating standout scripts by elevating story. The secret to telling strong story is digging deep inside yourself and utilizing your own life experiences and emotions to connect with the audience. As a television executive, the author asked writers about their personal stories and found that many writers had powerful life experiences, yet had surprisingly never drawn upon these for the sake of their writing because these experiences seemed to hit a little too close to home. This book is about jumping over that hurdle. The goal is not to write a straight autobiographical story which rarely transfers well. Rather, the intention is to dig deep into your well of experience, examine what you have inside, and use it to strengthen your writing. By doing so, you will be able to sell your scripts, find representation, be hired, and win writing competitions.

"Jen Grisanti has spent her entire professional life around writers and writing. Her new book is nothing less than an instruction manual, written from her unique perspective as a creative executive, that seeks to teach neophyte writers how to access their own experiences as fuel for their television and motion picture scripts. It aspires to be for writers what 'the Method' is for actors."

– Glenn Gordon Caron, writer/creator, *Moonlighting, Clean and Sober, Picture Perfect, Love Affair, Medium*

"Jen Grisanti gets to the heart of what makes us want to be storytellers in the first place – to share something of ourselves and touch the spirits of others in the process. Her book is a powerful and compassionate guide to discovering and developing stories that will enable us to connect – with an audience and with each other."

– Diane Drake, writer, *What Women Want, Only You*

JEN GRISANTI is a story consultant, independent producer, and the writing instructor for NBC's Writers on the Verge. She was a television executive for 12 years at top studios. She started her career in television and rose through the ranks of Current Programs at Spelling Television Inc. where Aaron Spelling was her mentor for 12 years.

$26.95 · 250 PAGES · ORDER NUMBER 156RLS · ISBN 13: 9781932907896

HOLLYWOOD GAME PLAN

HOW TO LAND A JOB IN FILM, TV, OR DIGITAL ENTERTAINMENT

CAROLE M. KIRSCHNER

Hollywood Game Plan is an in-depth, how-to guide for aspiring Hollywood hopefuls. It provides a concrete, step-by-step strategy to land a job in the entertainment industry. It is the first book to provide insights and advice from both sides of the spectrum: seasoned professionals with decades-long success and wisdom, and up-and-coming professionals who were pounding the pavement just a few years ago and share the up-to-the minute strategies that helped them land their first jobs. *Hollywood Game Plan* is unique in its teaching approach. Other books instruct readers to follow up with an email after a general meeting. This book tells readers exactly what to write in the subject line of the email, when to send it, and how long to wait before sending another one. Other books advise readers to dress nicely for interviews. Only *Hollywood Game Plan* describes specific outfits and accessories that can make the difference between a so-so interview and a successful one. No other book provides these types of details from successful professionals who know first hand why they work.

"Get Hollywood Game Plan, *study it, and use it like a bible to chart your course through the murky, shark-infested waters of the Hollywood media industry. From her positions in many aspects of the business, including quite a few at the top, Carole has seen what works and what does not. Her generosity in passing along this wisdom should not be wasted. If you want to break in and move up the food chain of Hollywood, start with Carole's book.*"

– Pamela Jaye Smith, author, international speaker and consultant, award-winning producer-director, MYTHWORKS founder, and Alpha Babe Academy co-founder

Sixteen years as a successful senior-level Hollywood executive – including stints at CBS and Steven Spielberg's Amblin Television – have honed CAROLE M. KIRSCHNER's ability to translate the unwritten rules of show business into plain English. She was involved in developing *Murphy Brown*, *Designing Women*, *Steven Spielberg Presents Tiny Toon Adventures*, *Reboot*, and the original *La Femme Nikita* series, and now develops and runs innovative entertainment industry training programs for the WGA Showrunner Training Program, CBS Diversity Institute Writers Mentoring Program, and the Hollywood Assistant Training Program. She also leads popular seminars on Hollywood pitching and networking, and through her private career consulting practice teaches clients exactly what they need to do to succeed in Hollywood. Carole is proud to have helped launch the careers of more than a hundred entertainment professionals and looks forward to helping many more.

$26.95 · 200 PAGES · ORDER NUMBER 178RLS · ISBN: 9781615930869

THE MYTH OF MWP

In a dark time, a light bringer came along, leading the curious and the frustrated to clarity and empowerment. It took the well-guarded secrets out of the hands of the few and made them available to all. It spread a spirit of openness and creative freedom, and built a storehouse of knowledge dedicated to the betterment of the arts.

The essence of the Michael Wiese Productions (MWP) is empowering people who have the burning desire to express themselves creatively. We help them realize their dreams by putting the tools in their hands. We demystify the sometimes secretive worlds of screenwriting, directing, acting, producing, film financing, and other media crafts.

By doing so, we hope to bring forth a realization of 'conscious media' which we define as being positively charged, emphasizing hope and affirming positive values like trust, cooperation, self-empowerment, freedom, and love. Grounded in the deep roots of myth, it aims to be healing both for those who make the art and those who encounter it. It hopes to be transformative for people, opening doors to new possibilities and pulling back veils to reveal hidden worlds.

MWP has built a storehouse of knowledge unequaled in the world, for no other publisher has so many titles on the media arts. Please visit www.mwp.com where you will find many free resources and a 25% discount on our books. Sign up and become part of the wider creative community!

Onward and upward,

Michael Wiese
Publisher/Filmmaker